USING CP/M®

by
JUDI N. FERNANDEZ
RUTH ASHLEY
Co-Presidents
DuoTech

John Wiley & Sons, Inc., Publishers
New York • Chichester • Brisbane • Toronto

Library of Congress Cataloging in Publication Data:

Fernandez, Judi N 1941-
Using CP/M.®

(Wiley Self-Teaching Guides)
1. CP/M (Computer program) 2. Microcomputers — Programming. I. Ashley, Ruth, joint author. II. Title.
QA76.6.F46 001.64'2 80-36673
ISBN 0-471-08011-X

Printed in the United States of America

81 80 10 9 8 7 6 5 4 3 2 1

To Peggy Kolbe, who supports all our writing efforts

Acknowledgments

Our thanks

to Bill Gutz and Walt Jellison, who sold us CP/M,

to Paul Ward, who helped us get our early versions running,

to P. Scot McIntosh, who provided technical assistance and reviews while we wrote this book,

to Mary Hoogterp and Donna Tabler, for testing the content, and

to Barbara Tabler, for typing the manuscript and trying out our answers whenever she didn't believe them.

To The Reader

About CP/M

CP/M – Control Program/Microcomputers – is a disk operating system for microcomputers based on the 8080, 8085, and the Z-80 type microprocessor chip. It is a software package developed and distributed by Digital Research of Pacific Grove, CA. It has become the most common microcomputer operating system and many other commercially available software packages are written to run under CP/M.

An operating system is a set of programs that helps you operate the computer and perform routine work functions. The CP/M system includes programs that allow you to run other programs, create files, erase files, copy files, translate, and test 8080 Assembler language programs, print data from files, display the directory of a disk, and so on. Without CP/M or a similar operating system, it would be very difficult and tedious for you to perform even the most trivial task on your computer.

This book assumes that you have a microcomputer and a CP/M package. Our intent is not to help you select a system, but to help you use what you already have. If you do not yet have your system, but have selected the machine and CP/M, you will still benefit from studying this book. You will need to skip the machine exercises and come back to them when your system has been installed.

This book presents the basic CP/M package delivered by Digital Research. Your hardware manufacturer may have adapted CP/M to fit the features of its equipment. They will, however, most likely have added functions. Therefore everything presented in this book should work on your system no matter what hardware you are using. For extra features study the manuals that arrive with your system – after you have finished this book.

There have been several versions of CP/M released by Digital Research. Each new release is an upgrade of earlier releases. Nothing is lost,but some features may have been changed as well as new features added. This book is current with release 2.0. However, we will warn you of differences from earlier versions.

About the Authors

The authors have published more than 100 computer-related instructional courses. We use CP/M daily in our own work and have a great deal of practical experience in using it and in explaining it to others. Our small business system consists of an Altos CPU, two Shugart disk drives, Perkin-Elmer Fox terminal, and Diablo printer. On a daily basis our system is used for word processing, COBAL, FORTRAN, BASIC, Assembler, and Pascal programming.

How to Use This Book

This Self-Teaching Guide consists of 10 chapters that have been carefully sequenced to introduce you to CP/M and to help you to develop a useful set of skills. We have made every effort to organize the material in the best possible learning sequence, so that you can begin using CP/M as quickly as possible. We strongly recommend that you study the chapters in order. You will learn to do easy tasks, then successively more complex tasks, until you have mastered the system.

Each chapter begins with a short introduction followed by objectives that outline what you can expect to learn from it, and ends with a Self-Test which allows you to measure your learning and practice what you have studied. Each chapter also contains a Suggested Machine Exercise that guides you in transferring your new knowledge to the real, hands-on environment.

The body of each chapter is divided into frames – short numbered sections in which information is presented or reviewed, followed by questions which ask you to apply the information. The correct answers to these questions follow a dashed line after the frame. As you work through the book, use a folded paper or a card to cover the correct answer until you have written yours. And be sure you actually write each response, especially when the activity is coding CP/M commands. Only by actually writing out the commands, and checking them carefully, can you get the most from this Self-Teaching Guide.

And don't worry! There's almost nothing you can do, apart from outright physical abuse, that can damage your system. Certainly there's no command you can enter that will hurt either CP/M or the hardware. At the most, you can lose some data, and that's what this book and the Suggested Machine Exercises will help to prevent.

For the proper physical care of your system see your manufacturer's recommendations.

Contents

CHAPTER ONE

Introduction to CP/M

CP/M is a set of programs that runs a microcomputer. To be more specific, CP/M enables *you* to control the operation of a microcomputer.

Before you can learn to use CP/M, you need to have some background information. What major components does the microcomputer have? What major components does CP/M have? How do the components of both interact to produce a functioning system? This introductory chapter will answer these questions for you as it introduces some of the terminology used in the computer world.

When you have finished this chapter, you will be able to:

- identify the required components of a microcomputer under CP/M,
- identify the functions of the major parts of a CP/M system,
- specify names for disk drives,
- recognize valid filenames,
- show how to select a given disk drive,
- interpret error messages that may result from drive selection.

MICROCOMPUTER COMPONENTS

The microcomputer controlled by CP/M typically includes main memory, a console, a printer, and at least one disk drive. We'll look at these components before we talk about what CP/M does with them.

1. A microprocessor that is to use CP/M must have at least 20K bytes of *main memory.* Main memory is the storage area inside the computer itself as opposed to *external storage* on your disks or tape. It is contained inside your computer just as the Z80 or 8080 or 8085 chip is. In order for any program to run on your computer it must be stored in main memory. (This includes the CP/M programs.)

In computer terms, "K" refers to about one thousand – actually 1024 – so 20K means more than 20,000. A *byte* is the amount of storage space required to store one character of data. So CP/M requires enough main memory in the microcomputer to store at least 20,000 characters. Most microcomputers that run under CP/M have more memory – 32K is common but many have 48K, 64K or more. Early versions of CP/M could run with as little as 16K bytes.

(a) What term refers to the amount of storage needed to store one letter, such as "B"? ______

(b) How would you specify that a microprocessor has room for about 32 thousand characters? ______

(c) Would the microprocessor in (b) above be large enough to handle CP/M? ______

(d) What's the difference between main memory and external storage? ______

______

______

- - - - - - - - - - - - - - - -

(a) byte; (b) 32k bytes; (c) yes; (d) main memory is inside the computer; external storage is on an outside device like disk or tape

2. The microcomputer system that is to use CP/M must have at least one *disk drive.* The drive supports one of various types of disks. The most common is the 8-inch *floppy disk.* This is a flexible disk encased in a stiff paper envelope. A 5½-inch diameter "mini-floppy" disk is used in some microcomputers. Aside from their size, the floppy disks look and work much the same. The floppy disks come in single- or double-sided, single- or double-density formatted. A single-sided, single-density 8-inch disk holds 256K bytes of data. A double-sided, double-density 8-inch disk holds up to four times as much. A single-sided, single-density 5-½ inch disk holds 72K bytes. Some microcomputers use a "hard disk". This provides even more storage and is also supported by CP/M.

The disk drive determines the type of diskette you use. If you have a drive designed to handle 8-inch, single-density, single-sided diskettes, then you can't put any other type of diskette in that drive.

Whatever type of disk drive your microcomputer has, CP/M requires at least one. The maximum number of drive, depends on your specific CP/M package, and we'll discuss that later.

(a) Are disk drives used for main memory or external storage? ______

______

(b) How many disk drives are required by CP/M? ______

(c) Does CP/M require any particular type of disk drive? ______

(d) What type of disk has more storage available at a time – a 5-½ inch, an 8-inch disk, or a hard disk? ______

- - - - - - - - - - - - - - - -

(a) external storage; (b) at least one; (c) no; (d) hard disk has more

3. CP/M also requires one *console* device for communication purposes. One type of console is the *teletype-style console.* It looks pretty much like a typewriter, with a keyboard and a printing unit. You "talk" to CP/M by typing on the keyboard. CP/M echoes what you type on the printer so that you can see what you're typing. (This is a major difference from a regular typewriter, where the keyboard directly controls the printer. Under CP/M it may look like you're typing directly on the printer, but in fact CP/M is in between.)

Another common type of console is the *video terminal.* This terminal includes a TV-like screen and a typewriter-like keyboard. You communicate with the microcomputer by typing at the keyboard. CP/M communicates with you by displaying messages on the console screen.

The console keyboard is arranged basically like typewriter keys, but it usually includes extra letters and symbols such as brackets ([,]) and other signs (for example < and >). It also contains special keys. The most important one for the CP/M user is the *control key.* It may be labeled CTL, CNTL, CTRL, or CONTROL. This key is crucial to using CP/M. You'll be very familiar with the control key by the time you finish this book.

(a) How many consoles does CP/M require? ________________

(b) Does CP/M require a teletypewriter or a video console? ________________

(c) At the console, the letters you type appear on the display device (video screen or printer). What causes the letters to be displayed? ________________

____

(d) Name one special key that is needed for CP/M. ________________

- - - - - - - - - - - - - - - -

(a) one; (b) either; (c) CP/M reads and echoes each character; (d) control key

4. The microprocessor, the disk drives, and the console are frequently supplemented with a *line printer* or list device. The printer is used for making "hard copy" versions of files and data from the disks, and for output from programs run on the microcomputer.

CP/M does not require a line printer. If you have a teletype-style console, you probably won't have a separate line printer. If you have a video console, you may also have a line printer.

Which of the following hardware devices are *required* by CP/M?

________ (a) At least 20K of main memory.

________ (b) A console device.

________ (c) A line printer.

_______ (d) At least one tape device.

_______ (e) At least one disk device.

- - - - - - - - - - - - - - - - -

a, b, e

5. A *peripheral device* is a device attached to the microprocessor, but not part of it. Each disk drive, the console, and the line printer are all considered separate peripheral devices even though several of them may be physically part of the same piece of equipment. Other peripheral equipment may be present as well. For example, some microcomputers may read or punch a paper tape, or use cassette tapes in addition to disks for storage. These can also be handled by CP/M as peripheral devices. When CP/M is first installed on a new system, it is tailored so it knows what peripheral devices are attached.

Match the items below with descriptive phrases on the right:

_______	(a) main memory	(1) peripheral device
_______	(b) printer	(2) essential to CP/M
_______	(c) disk drive	
_______	(d) console	
_______	(e) tape drive	

- - - - - - - - - - - - - - - - -

(a) 2; (b) 1; (c) 1, 2; (d) 1, 2; (e) 1

6. CP/M monitors a microcomputer system made up of various pieces of equipment, which is called *hardware.* CP/M itself, however, is *software.* That is, CP/M consists of programs of data, not equipment. CP/M is an *operating system;* it is a system of programs that allow you to operate your computer. The software provided by CP/M lets the microprocessor know what peripheral devices are available and acts as an interface between the microprocessor and you. It also acts as an interface between any two peripheral devices, or between the microprocessor and any attached device.

Which of the following are functions or features of CP/M?

_______ (a) serves as a hardware device

_______ (b) interfaces between pieces of hardware

_______ (c) operating system

_______ (d) software

- - - - - - - - - - - - - - - - -

b, c, d

THE CP/M PROGRAMS

We have said several times that CP/M is a *set* of programs. In the frames that follow, we'll overview the major CP/M programs.

7. The *Functional Disk Operating System* (FDOS) is the portion of CP/M that handles all input and output between main memory and the peripheral devices. FDOS is usually pronounced as "F-doss," or "F-doz."

FDOS is a set of programs that supports any other program that requires input or output services. If you were writing a program to print data on a line printer, you could write your own output routines. However, you could save yourself a lot of time and trouble by simply calling on FDOS to do the work for you.

All the other CP/M programs use FDOS to read input or write output.

Which of the following functions would be handled by FDOS?

_______ (a) Write data on a disk.

_______ (b) Arithmetic calculations.

_______ (c) Read data from the console.

_______ (d) Read data from a disk.

_______ (e) Write data on the line printer.

- - - - - - - - - - - - - - - - -

a, c, d, e

8. FDOS consists of two parts: the basic input/output system (BIOS), and the basic disk operating system (BDOS). We'll look at these parts separately.

The *basic input/output system* (BIOS) handles the transfer of data between any peripheral device (except the disk) and the microprocessor. BIOS is usually pronounced "BY-ose."

BIOS handles these functions:

- locates the correct device,
- checks to see if the device is busy and if so, waits until it's free,
- checks the device for any hardware malfunction,
- transfers the data to or from the device at the correct speed for that device,
- checks the transferred data for any obvious errors.

(a) What does BIOS stand for? _______________

(b) What is the basic function of BIOS? _______________

____

(c) What CP/M program is BIOS part of? _______________

____

____

(d) A typical line printer can receive data at a speed of 120 characters per second. A typical video console can receive characters at a speed of 960 characters per second. What CP/M program is responsible for sending data to each device at the correct speed? ______

(a) basic input/output system; (b) transfer data between main memory and peripheral devices; (c) FDOS; (d) BIOS

9. The *basic disk operating system* (BDOS) controls the organization of data on a disk. BDOS is usually pronounced "B-doss" or "B-doz."

Data is kept on disk in files. A file is a set of related data. For example, your office might have a payroll file that contains the payroll information for all your company's employees. This file, in turn, contains records. For the payroll file there would be one record for each employee that would contain an employee's name, address, wage rate, tax rate, and so forth.

The payroll file is an example of a data file. Another type of file you will have is a program file, which contains all the commands that make up one computer program. Each command is a record.

One disk may contain many files. It's not unusual to have more than 50 files on one disk. BDOS keeps track of all the files on the disk.

(a) What do the letters BDOS stand for? ______

(b) What CP/M program is BDOS a part of? ______

(c) What is the basic function of BDOS? ______

______

The diagram below depicts the structure of a disk. Label the three levels as file, disk, or record.

(d) ______

(e) ______

(f) ______

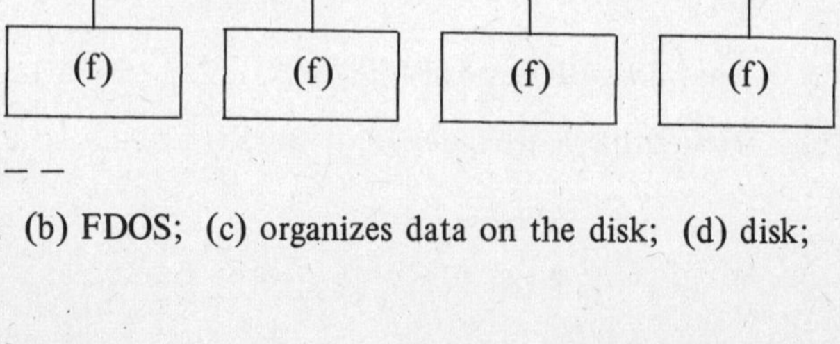

(a) basic disk operating system; (b) FDOS; (c) organizes data on the disk; (d) disk; (e) file; (f) record

10. Every file must have a name. BDOS keeps a file *directory* on each disk. The directory shows all the file names, their sizes, and their exact locations on the disk.

Every time you add a new file to a disk BDOS does the following:

- checks the directory to make sure there is no file with the same name,
- checks the directory to make sure there is room for the file,
- updates the directory with an entry for the new file.

(a) What CP/M program maintains the disk directory? ______________________

(b) What information does the disk directory contain? ______________________

____

____

- - - - - - - - - - - - - - - -

(a) BDOS; (b) file name, file size, file location

11. Suppose you want to type out a file from disk to your line printer. Identify whether BIOS or BDOS handles each of the following functions.

(a) Locates the correct disk drive. ______________________

(b) Waits until the disk drive is ready. ______________________

(c) Checks the disk directory to find the location of the file. ______________

(d) Waits until the printer is ready. ______________________

(e) Transfers the data from the disk to the printer. ______________________

- - - - - - - - - - - - - - - -

(a) BIOS; (b) BIOS; (c) BDOS; (d) BIOS; (e) BIOS

12. The preceding frames have discussed the FDOS and its two major parts, BIOS and BDOS. Another major set of CP/M programs is the *console command processor* (CCP). This is the part you will use directly. The CCP reads whatever you type on the console and processes the commands you give it. Everytime you interact with CP/M you use the CCP. You can enter commands to list a directory or erase a file and CCP will process the command and do as you ask. You can request processing external to CCP, and the CCP will handle the request and then return to you. All your commands at the console are handled through the CCP of CP/M.

(a) What does CCP stand for? ______________________

(b) Can you interact with CP/M without using the CCP? ______________

If so, how? ______________________

- - - - - - - - - - - - - - - -

____

(a) console command processor; (b) no

13. The CCP program contains several routines for functions that you will use all the time. You will learn how to use the functions in Chapter 3, but we'll overview them here:

- DIR displays the directory of a disk,
- ERA erases a file from a disk.
- TYPE displays a file.
- SAVE writes data from main memory to a disk file.
- REN renames a file.
- USER changes the user number (version 2.0 and up).

Because these functions are part of the CCP, they're always available to you whenever CP/M is running on your computer. Therefore they're called *built-in programs.* The commands that you type to use them (DIR, ERA, etc.) are called the built-in commands.

(a) What major CP/M program contains the built-in programs? ______________

(b) To use a built-in program, you type a built-in ________________ on your console.

(c) If your computer is on but you haven't loaded CP/M into main memory, would the built-in commands work? __________ Why? ________________

____

\- - - - - - - - - - - - - - - -

(a) CCP; (b) command; (c) no, because they're part of CP/M

14. The other CP/M programs you are studying in this section, such as BIOS and BDOS, are also built into the CP/M package. Whenever CP/M is running on your system, they are automatically stored in main memory and are available to CP/M. However, you have no commands to use them. They are only called by other programs. For example, CCP uses BIOS to communicate with your console.

Even though they are built-in programs, they have no matching built-in commands.

Match the functions below with their characteristics.

______ (a) CCP, FDOS, BIOS	1. Built-in program
______ (b) DIR, ERA, TYPE	2. Built-in command
	3. Always available when CP/M is running

\- - - - - - - - - - - - - - - -

(a) 1, 3; (b) 1, 2, 3

15. Any program that is not built-in is called a *transient program.* The term "transient" refers to the fact that the program is only loaded into main memory when it is needed. A transient program is kept in a file on disk. Its filename becomes the command that you type if you want to use the program.

Your CP/M system disk contains several transient programs provided by Digital Research. You might also buy other transient programs from other sources or write your own.

There are only a few built-in commands, but you can have as many transient commands as you can fit files on a disk.

Match the program types on the left with their descriptions on the right.

_______ (a) built-in program

_______ (b) transient program

1. Only stored in main memory when needed.
2. Always in main memory when CP/M is running.
3. You can write one.
4. You can buy one and add it to your system.
5. Part of CP/M package from Digital Research

- - - - - - - - - - - - - - - -

(a) 2, 5; (b) 1, 3, 4, 5

16. The built-in programs are always in main memory whenever CP/M is running. A transient program must be loaded into main memory from disk each time it is used.

Which type of programs do you think would be faster to run? _______________

_______________ Why? _______________________________

- - - - - - - - - - - - - - - -

Built-in programs; because there's no loading time

17. (a) Give an example of a built-in program that has no matching built-in command. _______________________________

(b) Which CP/M program contains the built-in programs? _______________

(c) A program that's loaded from disk into main memory each time it's used is called a _______________________________

(d) Which type of program is faster? _______________________

- - - - - - - - - - - - - - - -

(a) you might have said CCP, FDOS, BDOS, or BIOS; (b) CCP; (c) transient program; (d) built-in

CP/M ARCHITECTURE

You have seen the major built-in programs of CP/M – FDOS, which contains BDOS and BIOS, and CCP. The following section explains how CP/M organizes your computer's main memory to allow for both built-in programs and transient programs.

18. The diagram on the right shows how CP/M organizes your computer's main memory. You can see where FDOS and CCP are stored.

The *transient program area* (TPA) holds all transient programs and data you are using.

The sizes of the FDOS and CCP areas are fixed. They're large enough to hold those programs. The size of your TPA equals your computer's main memory size minus the sizes of CCP, FDOS, BOOT, and the system area. So the TPA size varies from system to system. Refer to the diagram above to answer these questions.

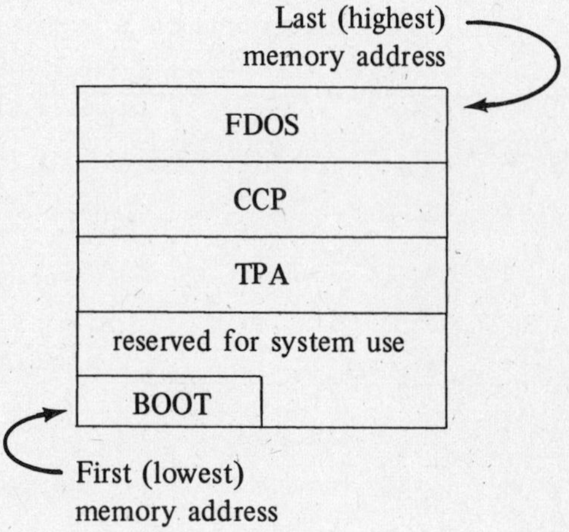

(a) CCP is in the (lowest/highest) ________________ part of memory.

(b) The size of CCP is (fixed/variable) ________________________________.

(c) The size of FDOS is (fixed/variable) ______________________________.

(d) The size of the TPA is (fixed/variable) ____________________________.

(e) Suppose your system has 32K bytes of memory. Suppose also that the reserved area, FDOS, and CCP take up 6K bytes. How large is your TPA? ______________

- - - - - - - - - - - - - - - - -

(a) highest; (b) fixed; (c) fixed; (d) variable; (e) 26K bytes

19. *Boot,* the program in the lowest part of memory, has a very special function. Since the CCP is higher than the TPA in memory, and since the TPA can vary in size, CP/M needs to know exactly where to find the beginning of CCP. BOOT is a very small program that tells CP/M where CCP is.

Whenever you start up the system, control goes to the part of main memory where BOOT is. BOOT reads the entire CP/M system into memory. It then transfers control to the BIOS. We often think of BOOT as kicking (or "booting") control to the beginning of the CP/M system. CCP takes over and you're ready to go.

Some transient programs might also use the FDOS and CCP areas in memory. If this happens, then FDOS and CCP need to be reloaded from disk before CP/M can continue. Such transient programs end by transferring control to BOOT. BOOT causes CCP and FDOS to be reloaded then transfers control to the beginning of CCP.

(a) BOOT is located at the (beginning/end) __________ of main memory.

(b) Among other things, BOOT contains the beginning address of __________.

(c) When you start up your system, control goes first to __________.

- - - - - - - - - - - - - - - -

(a) beginning; (b) BIOS; (c) BOOT

Now you know that CP/M is an operating system. It drives a microcomputer system that includes at least 20K of main memory and various peripheral devices. These peripherals include a console, at least one disk drive, and perhaps others as well. CP/M itself is made up of the full disk operating system, which includes the BIOS and BDOS, the console command processor (CCP), the transient program area (TPA), and the BOOT.

Now we're going to look more closely at some items that you'll be using under CP/M: the disks, the disk drives, and the files that reside on the disks.

DISK DRIVES

20. CP/M comes in several versions; the most common are version 1.4 and 2.2. CP/M 1.4 supports one to four disk drives. CP/M versions later than 2.0 support up to 16 drives. The principles are the same in both systems.

As you know, various types of disk drives can be supported by CP/M. These drives have individual names within the CP/M system. Drives are named in alphabetical order. Thus, the primary drive is named "A" and the secondary drive is named "B".

(a) What is the highest possible drive name in version 1.4 CP/M? __________

(b) What is the highest possible drive name in version 2.0 CP/M? __________

- - - - - - - - - - - - - - - -

(a) D; (b) P

21. The exact method for turning on CP/M varies with the hardware involved. But no matter how it's done, the CCP gives you your first message like this:

```
64K CP/M VERSION 2.2

A>_
```

This symbol represents the cursor.

The first line tells you the size of the CP/M system on your A disk. The second line (A>) tells you two things: the CCP is ready to receive a command, and the currently selected disk drive is A. The currently selected drive is also called the active or default drive. CP/M always starts up on drive A. You can select another disk drive, and change the active drive, by entering the desired drive name followed by a colon. If you type this:

A>B:

and press return, the CCP responds with this:

B>_

Now the B drive is active and the CCP is ready for another command.

(a) Given the prompt below, which drive is active?

B>_

____

(b) How can you make "D" the active drive? ____________________

(c) How can you select drive A? ____________________

(d) When CP/M is started, which disk drive is selected for you? __________

- - - - - - - - - - - - - - - -

(a) drive B; (b) enter D:; (c) enter A:; (d) drive A

22. If you select a drive your setup doesn't have, CP/M can't select it. Suppose you have a two-drive system and you enter:

```
A>C:
```

CP/M will give you an error message. The standard message looks like this:

```
BDOS ERROR ON C: SELECT_
```

Any character from the keyboard will cause CP/M to boot and give you the prompt again. Under the standard CP/M you'll get that same message for any invalid drive name with the invalid drive name repeated in the message.

Some manufacturers have modified CP/M and illegal drive names may end in a cryptic message – like TRANSIENT DISK ERROR #80 – or even hang up the system. You may have to restart to get the system working again. You'll want to try this on your machine to see exactly what happens.

Sometimes you may select a legal drive but not have a disk loaded. This will cause a system hang-up under standard CP/M – CP/M will just wait until a disk is inserted or until you boot the system. Some hardware manufacturers have modified this and you may get some more specific, or more cryptic information.

Suppose you are using a CP/M version 1.4 system that has a disk in each of the two disk drives. You start it up and get A>. What happens for each entry below?

(a) A>B: ______________________________

(b) A>D: ______________________________

(c) A>G: ______________________________

(d) A>A: ______________________________

(a) the B drive is selected;
(b) BDOS ERROR ON D: SELECT;
(c) BDOS ERROR ON G: SELECT;
(d) drive A remains active

23. The colon is a critical part of drive selection. If you enter a drive name without the colon, the CCP doesn't know you want to select a drive. It thinks you want to run a program of that name. If it can't find any program with that name, you'll get a message like this:

```
A>B
B?

A>_
```

The prompt you get always indicates the active drive. Because the CP/M system didn't recognize B as a drive name, the current drive remained active.

For each example below tell what might have happened.

(a)
```
A>B:
BDOS ERROR ON B: SELECT_
```

____

(b)
```
A>B:
B>_
```

____

____

(c)
```
A>H:
BDOS ERROR ON H: SELECT_
```

(d)
```
A>C
C?

A>_
```

- - - - - - - - - - - - - - - -

(a) either the system has only one disk drive or the B drive has no disk in it;
(b) drive B was selected;
(c) either there is no H drive or the H drive has no disk in it;
(d) the colon was omitted and drive A remains active; also, no program named C exists on drive A

DISKS

24. Disks used by CP/M systems are specific to the drives used. They are often described as being "IBM-compatible" because of their format. Each disk is divided into tracks and sectors, as you can see here. The number of tracks and sectors depends on the size and type of disk. A typical 8-inch disk contains 77 tracks and is divided into 26 sectors. The *tracks* are concentric rings. The *sectors* form wedges that intersect with the tracks. You can see that sector 20, track 12, could be used to refer to a specific part of the disk. (You won't have to do this, but the BDOS does when it locates files or data.) Sometimes when CP/M finds a disk error, it may tell you the track or sector involved.

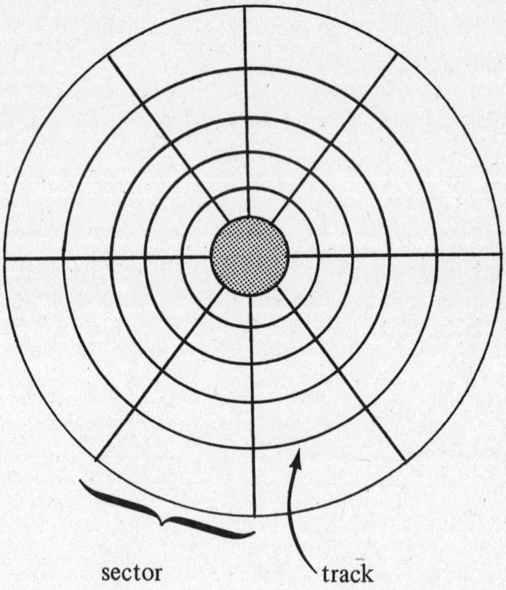

The track nearest the outside edge is track 0, and the next is track 1. The entire CP/M system, including FDOS and CCP, generally resides on these two tracks of an 8-inch diskette. When you start up CP/M, the entire system is loaded (or copied) into main memory. The rest of the disk is available to store transient programs and your files.

(a) What is the difference between a track and a sector? ______________________

____

(b) What tracks or sectors contain the CP/M system on an 8-inch diskette? ________

____

(c) Suppose a disk has 77 tracks. How many are available for transient programs and files? ____

- - - - - - - - - - - - - - - - -

(a) tracks are concentric rings and sectors are wedges; (b) tracks zero and one; (c) 75

25. The system tracks contain all the CP/M built-in programs: the BIOS and BDOS, CCP, and BOOT. BDOS puts the directory on the first track after the system tracks. (Under version 2.2, your system may be modified to use more than two tracks. However, the system tracks will still act as a whole.) BDOS sets up the directory as files are added to the disk. It keeps track of what files are on the disk and where they are. You'll learn to use the directory later in this book.

Which of the following are physically located in the system tracks of a CP/M disk?

_______ (a) BDOS

_______ (b) BIOS

_______ (c) CCP

_______ (d) TPA

_______ (e) BOOT

_______ (f) directory

_______ (g) data files

- - - - - - - - - - - - - - - - -

a, b, c, e

FILES

26. A *file* on a CP/M disk is a set of information. It may be a program, information, or such items as letters or reports. A file is anything you have called a file and stored on a CP/M disk.

Every file on a disk has a unique name with two or three parts. Here's an example of a *filename:*

A:CHAP1.PRN

Let's look at the parts of this name separately.

The first part is the drivename. This part of the filename may vary, depending on which drive the disk is placed. It's not a *permanent* part of the filename. If used, it's followed by a colon.

The second part is the filename proper. It has from one to eight characters and must start with a letter. The third part is the filetype. It has from zero to three characters. Every file doesn't need a filetype. But if one is used, it is separated from the filename proper with a period.

If you type a filename longer than eight characters or a filetype longer than three characters, CP/M truncates (chops off) the extra characters. Thus, WEDNESDAYS. MENUS will be read as WEDNESDA.MEN.

Indicate if each name below is a valid CP/M filename. If not, state why it is invalid.

(a) A:FILE6

valid ____________ invalid ______________________________

(b) FILE6.SIX

valid ____________ invalid ______________________________

(c) 6FILE.SIX

valid ____________ invalid ______________________________

(d) FILESIXTEEN

valid ____________ invalid ______________________________

(e) A

valid ____________ invalid ______________________________

- - - - - - - - - - - - - - - -

(a) valid; (b) valid; (c) invalid (doesn't begin with a letter); (d) this is valid but will be read as FILESIXT; (e) valid (but could be confused with drive A:)

27. The filename and filetype may be determined by the user. But CP/M recognizes certain filetypes and may treat them differently. Here are a few of the standard filetypes.

$$$	CP/M uses this to indicate a temporary file.
COM	A CP/M command file; a file with this filetype is run as a transient program.
PRN	A print file; a file with filetype PRN can usually be printed out directly.

BAK	A backup file; CP/M programs create these automatically under certain conditions.
COB FOR BAS ASM PLI PLM	These represent computer source programs in various languages – COBOL, Fortran, Basic, Assembler, PL/I and PL/M.

CP/M has other standard filetypes also. Many files will have filetypes needed by your transient programs. You may have inventory data of type INV, correspondence files of type COR, and extra files of type X. Or you may not use filetypes for many of your files.

Indicate if each filetype below is valid or invalid. If it is invalid tell why.

(a) COM

valid ________ invalid ____________________

(b) COMMAND

valid ________ invalid ____________________

(c) DOC

valid ________ invalid ____________________

(d) 6X

valid ________ invalid ____________________

- - - - - - - - - - - - - - -

(a) valid; (b) valid but will be read as COM; (c) valid; (d) valid

28. Each combination of filename and filetype on a disk must be unique. That means you may have several files named TEXT1 on a disk if each has a different filetype. You may also have several files of the same type as long as each has a different filename. The drivename may be the same for each file on the same disk. You can use the same filename-filetype combination on many different disks because you'll never have two disks on the same disk drive at once.

Which of the sets of complete filenames below represent unique names?

______	(a) A:TEXT1.DOC A:TEXT1.BAK A:TEXT1	______	(c) A:TEXT3.DOC B:TEXT3.DOC B:TEXT3.BAK
______	(b) A:TEXT2.DOC A:TEXT2 A:TEXT2	______	(d) B:TEXT4.DOC B:TEXT3.DOC A:TEXT4.DOC

- - - - - - - - - - - - - - -

a, c, d

29. CP/M allows you to protect your important disks from being written on. You can give any drive, except the A drive, *read/only* status. This means that you can read any file on the disk, but you can't write on it. When a disk is read/only, you can't add a new file, erase or change a file, or rename a file.

The opposite of read/only status is *read/write* status. This means that you can read files from a disk and write on any files on the disk.

You will learn how to assign read/only status and read/write status later in this book.

Match each status with its characteristics.

_______ (a) read/only

_______ (b) read/write

1. read files
2. erase files
3. change files
4. rename files
5. write new files

- - - - - - - - - - - - - - - -

(a) 1; (b) 1, 2, 3, 4, 5

30. With CP/M version 2.0, you can also assign read/only status to individual files. If you want to protect just one file on a disk, you can do so. You will learn how to do this later.

(a) What CP/M versions allow read/only status protection for an entire disk?

____

(b) What CP/M versions allow read/only status protection for individual files?

____

- - - - - - - - - - - - - - - -

(a) all versions; (b) 2.0 and later

In the previous section you have seen some special CP/M information about the disks, the disk drives, and the files on the disks. In the next section you'll learn how to start your CP/M system.

BOOTING

31. When you turn on your computer it may just sit there waiting for instructions. Before they can do anything, computers must have a program stored in main memory. Some computers have an automatic start capability. However, when using CP/M as your operating system, for most computers CP/M must be put into main memory. But

you have no command to do this since there is no program in memory to recognize and respond to a command.

The first program you load into memory each time you turn the power on must be bootstrapped in. That is, it must pull itself in. You'll have to learn how to do this for your computer. Usually it's a hardware function such as pushing a button or flipping a switch, and perhaps entering a trigger character. Check with your hardware manuals to find out.

Whatever the process, the system boot function will cause the system tracks from the disk on drive A to be read into main memory. If you're trying to load CP/M, the disk you put in drive A when you boot must contain the CP/M system programs on the system tracks.

A boot is also called a *"cold start"* because it's how you get the system started when it's completely cold; meaning that it contains no programs. After a cold start, control goes to the BOOT program which boots control to the CCP. This will give you a startup message telling your system size, followed by the CP/M prompt, A>.

(a) How do you get the first program into your computer's main memory after you turn the power on? ______________________________

(b) Describe the disk you must use to boot CP/M. ______________________________

____

What drive must it be on? ______________________________

(c) A system boot is also known as a ______________________________

(d) If you successfully boot CP/M, what message should appear on your console?

____

- - - - - - - - - - - - - - - -

(a) boot it in; (b) any disk containing the CP/M system programs on the system tracks, drive A; (c) cold start; (d) CP/M prompt (A>)

THE NEW CP/M SYSTEM

When you first get CP/M it must be tailored to your system. For example, BIOS needs to know exactly what peripheral devices you have. (After BIOS has been customized it's generally referred to as CBIOS, meaning "customized" BIOS.)

If your CP/M has not yet been tailored to your system, it must be done. Tailoring requires a knowledge of 8080 Assembler language and the hexadecimal number system. If you know these things, you can probably tailor your own system following the instructions in your CP/M Alteration Guide. If you don't, you'll need to get some help.

In the remainder of this book we're going to assume that your system has these features:

- video console,

- line printer,
- at least two floppy disk drives,
- no paper tape or magnetic tape devices.

This is the most common office microcomputer configuration. If your system is different, don't worry. The material you study here will still be valid, although the examples might be slightly different. Any time that we're discussing a command that is device dependent, we'll be sure to let you know.

This chapter has introduced you to the basic features of CP/M and the microcomputers that use CP/M. In the next chapter you'll begin learning how to enter a CP/M command. Before you start chapter 2, take the Self-Test and try your hand at the suggested machine exercises.

SELF-TEST

This Self-Test will help you determine if you have mastered the objectives of this chapter. Answer each question to the best of your ability, then check your answers in the answer key at the end of the test.

1. Which of the following are required components of a microcomputer under CP/M?

   ______ (a) main memory

   ______ (b) disk drives

   ______ (c) tape drives

   ______ (d) console

   ______ (e) paper tape reader

2. Identify the CP/M program that performs each function below:

   (a) interprets keyboard entries

   ____

   (b) performs file management

   ____

   (c) is customized to handle input and output operations

   ____

   (d) transfers control to the CCP

   ____

3. Under CP/M, what memory area is reserved for programs that are not built-in?

   ____

____

4. Suppose your screen shows this prompt:

```
A>_
```

(a) What is the active drive?

____

(b) How can you switch to drive B?

____

(c) What does it mean if CCP responds

```
BDOS ERROR ON B: SELECT_
```

____

(d) What does it mean if CCP responds

```
B?
A>_
```

____

5. Which of the complete filenames below represents a file of type COM, name STEST, on drive A?

_______ (a) A.COM.STEST

_______ (b) A.STEST.COM

_______ (c) A:STEST:COM

_______ (d) A:STEST.COM

6. Match each term below with its correct definition.

_______ (a) hardware

_______ (b) software

_______ (c) peripheral device

_______ (d) main memory

_______ (e) system tracks

(1) storage area in the computer's microprocessor

(2) screen on a video terminal

(3) any piece of input/output equipment

(4) zero and one

(5) any piece of equipment

(6) wedges of disk

(7) any computer program

Chapter 1 Answer Key

Compare your answers to the Self-Test with the correct answers given below. If all your answers are correct, you are ready to go on to the next chapter. If you missed any questions, you may find it helpful to review the appropriate frames before going on.

1. a, b, d

2. (a) console command processor (CCP)
   (b) basic disk operating system (BDOS)
   (c) basic input/output system (BIOS or CBIOS)
   (d) BOOT

3. transient program area (TPA)

4. (a) drive A
   (b) enter B:
   (c) either no drive B or no disk in drive B
   (d) you entered B without the colon

5. d

6. (a), (5)
   (b), (7)
   (c), (3)
   (d), (1)
   (e), (4)

Suggested Machine Exercises

Each chapter in this book ends with a suggested machine exercise. If you have your microcomputer and CP/M disk, we strongly recommend that you work these exercises. This is the best way to become comfortable with the CP/M system.

If you don't know how to boot your system, this first exercise is vital because every other exercise in this book starts by booting. Unfortunately we can't tell you how to boot because the process depends on your microcomputer.

1. Your system manual should tell you how to boot your system. If not, check with someone who would know, perhaps a colleague or your salesperson.

2. Turn the power on, load the system disk in drive A, and boot.

3. If you get no console message, try these things:
   a. check to see that your console is connected to the microprocessor and the power is on. If it's a separate device, it probably has a switch called LOCAL or LINE. Make sure this switch is in the LINE, not LOCAL, position,
   b. some systems need to warm up for a minute or two, so wait awhile and try again,
   c. if all else fails, get help.

4. If the boot succeeded, you should get a message something like this:

```
CP/M nnK VERS n.n

A>_
```

   nnK tells the size CP/M thinks your main memory is. Later in this book you'll learn how to change the size. VERS n.n tells you what version of CP/M you have.

5. Practice booting the system several times.

6. If you have more than one drive, install disks in the other drives and practice switching back and forth from one disk to another.

7. Try selecting a drive that contains no disk. You should get an error message, and you may have to boot to continue.

8. Try selecting drive Z:. You should get a BDOS error. Type any character to continue.

9. Shut down your system and go on to Chapter 2.

CHAPTER TWO

Typing CP/M Commands

You use CP/M programs by typing and entering commands. A typical command might be:

```
ERA JOHNSON.LET
```

This command asks CP/M to erase the disk file named JOHNSON.LET. There are many commands corresponding to the various CP/M built-in and transient programs. You'll be learning the command details in later chapters. In this chapter, we will cover the general format of all CP/M commands, what happens when a CP/M command is entered, and some special functions you can use when typing CP/M commands.

When you complete your study of this chapter, you will be able to:

- write a basic CP/M command involving a program and a file,
- write CP/M commands for programs that are not on the active drive,
- write CP/M commands for files that are not on the active drive,
- briefly describe what happens after a CP/M command is entered,
- given error messages resulting from CP/M commands, state the general cause of the error,
- identify the control characters that invoke major CP/M control functions.

GENERAL COMMAND FORMAT

1. In order to enter a CP/M command you must be at command level. This means you must have a CP/M prompt such as A>_.

The general format of a CP/M command is:

d>programname [operands] <carriage return>

The d> indicates the command prompt that's provided by the CCP.

Programname is the name of the program you want CP/M to execute. It must be either a built-in command or the name of a COM file (command file) on one of the drives.

A COM file is a transient program that has been translated into machine language and appropriately edited by the system so that it is completely ready to be run on your computer. Its filename will always be in this format: programname.COM. For example, your CP/M disk includes these transient program files: PIP.COM, ED.COM, STAT.COM.

In the CP/M command you only enter the programname; don't type the ".COM." Then you type the operands, if there are any. The command is terminated with a <carriage return>, which causes the CCP to process the command. The <carriage return> is a special key on your keyboard that may be labeled RETURN or ENTER.

(a) Before you can enter a CP/M command, what must appear on your terminal?

____

(b) Programname must be the name of:

______ a. a CP/M built-in command,

______ b. a COM file on one of the drives,

______ c. either of the above,

______ d. none of the above.

(c) Suppose your A disk contains these files: PIP.COM, STAT.COM, and TEST.COM.

You want to run the TEST program. What entry do you make? A>__________

- - - - - - - - - - - - - - - -

(a) CP/M prompt (d>); (b) c; (c) TEST

2. If the COM file is not on the active drive, you must tell CP/M where to find it. You can switch to the correct drive, as in:

```
A>B:
B>CALC
```

You can also precede the programname with the drivename, as in:

```
A>B:CALC
```

The major difference between these two techniques is the drive that remains active after the CALC program terminates. In the first example, the B drive remains active; in the second example, the A drive remains active. In the first example, B becomes the default for file references of CALC. In the second, A is default drive for file references of CALC even though CALC came from B disk.

For the following questions assume that your A disk contains PIP.COM, STAT.COM, and TEST.COM, and your B disk contains SORT.COM, MERGE.COM, and LIST.COM.

(a) Show the entry or entries you would make if you want to run the SORT program but leave the A drive active.

A> ____________________

(b) Show the entry or entries you would make if you want to run the LIST program and leave the B drive active.

A>

- - - - - - - - - - - - - - - -

(a) A>B:SORT; (b) A>B:
B>LIST

3. Here's the general command format again:

d>programname [operands] <carriage return>

Some programs do not involve operands. In these cases, just type the programname and press the carriage return key.

Many programs require a file as input. If so, type at least one space and then the filename as an operand, after the programname. If the file is on the active drive, you don't need to include the drivename. For example, if you want to erase the file named SOURCE.DAT from disk A, you could enter either of these commands:

A>ERA SOURCE.DAT
A>ERA A:SOURCE.DAT

If SOURCE.DAT is on disk B, you have three choices. You could switch the disks and reboot, but this isn't very practical. You could make drive B active, or you could enter this command:

A>ERA B:SOURCE.DAT

In most cases use the complete filename, including the filetype. We'll let you know when the filetype should be omitted.

(a) Show the general format for a CP/M command that does not require a filename.

d> ____________________

(b) Programname is separated from operands by ____________________

____________________.

(c) In a filename, the drivename is –

______ a. always needed

______ b. sometimes needed

______ c. never needed

(d) When a filename is an operand, do you generally include the filetype? ________

(e) Drive B is active. You want to erase the INVENTY.COM file on disk A. Show the fastest way to do this.

B>ERA ______________________________

- - - - - - - - - - - - - - - -

(a) programname; (b) one or more spaces; (c) b; (d) yes;
(e) B>ERA A:INVENTY.COM

4. The built-in commands must not be preceded by drivenames, as they are not related to drives. (Recall that they are part of the CCP.)

(a) Which of the following will type the file named INVENTY.DAT on drive B? (TYPE is a built-in command.)

______ a. A>TYPE B:INVENTY.DAT

______ b. A>B:TYPE INVENTY.DAT

______ c. A>B:
B>TYPE INVENTY.DAT

(b) Which of the following may not be prefixed with a drive name?

______ a. built-in commands

______ b. transient programnames

______ c. filenames

- - - - - - - - - - - - - - - -

(a) a, c; (b) a

5. For the questions below, assume that you have two disks containing these files:

Drive A	*Drive B*
SORT.COM	INVENTY.COM
MERGE.COM	INVENTY.DAT
SORT.DAT	PARTS.DAT

(a) Show the command(s) to run the SORT program using the file named PARTS.DAT as an operand. Leave control on drive A.

A> ______________________________

____

(b) Show the command(s) to erase SORT.DAT. (ERA is a built-in command.) Leave control on drive B.

B> ______________________________

____

(c) Show the command(s) to run the SORT program with INVENTY.DAT as an operand. Leave control on drive A.

B> ______________________________

____

- - - - - - - - - - - - - - - - -

(a) A>SORT B:PARTS.DAT; (b) B>ERA A:SORT.DAT;

(c) B>A:
A>SORT B:INVENTY.DAT

CP/M COMMAND PROCESSING

6. Now that you have seen what a CP/M command generally looks like, let's discuss what happens when you enter the command. First of all, CP/M searches for the program you named as programname. If it's a built-in program, it's already a part of the console command processor (CCP). It was loaded into main storage when the system was booted. Otherwise CP/M looks for the appropriate COM file on the disk on the specified drive. (If no drive was specified, the active drive is assumed.)

If it can't find the correct program, the CCP returns an error message – "programname?". CP/M does not search the other drives. Below is a sample printout in which we accidentally misspelled the ERA programname.

```
A>ERRA INVENTY.DAT
ERRA?

A>_
```

A message of one word followed by a question mark means the system can't recognize your programname. Either you misspelled it or the appropriate COM file is not on the specified drive.

The CP/M prompt is then repeated, as shown in the above example, so that you can enter the correct command. You'll have to type it over again; you can't go back and correct the earlier attempt.

(a) When you enter a CP/M command, what's the first thing the CCP does?

____

(b) Suppose you have the following interaction:

```
A>TYP JOHNSON.PRN
TYP?

A>_
```

What could be wrong?

______ a. TYP is not a built-in command.

______ b. JOHNSON.PRN is not a file on the A disk.

______ c. TYP.COM is not a file on the A disk.

- - - - - - - - - - - - - - - - - -

(a) CP/M searches for the programname program; (b) a and c

7. If the CCP successfully locates your transient program on the specified disk, it reads the program from the disk into the TPA. Depending on your hardware, you may be able to hear this happening. If it's a short program it could take less than a second to load. Longer programs may take five seconds or longer.

CCP also stores any operands in an area of main memory where the transient program can find them. Control is then given to the beginning of the program. You are now out of command level and into program level.

What happens next depends entirely on the program. Most programs will check the filename(s) and other operands, and display error messages if they aren't correct. You'll be learning more about this when you study the built-in commands and transient programs later on.

When the program terminates, CCP resumes control and you're back at command level again. You'll know when this occurs because you'll get the CP/M prompt.

(a) Below is shown a typical CP/M interaction.

```
A>COPY B A
        (3 SECOND WAIT)
A>_
```

Briefly describe what happened during the three second wait. (Note: COPY is not a built-in command.)

____

____

____

____

(b) Here's another interaction.

```
A>SORT INVENTY.DAT
FILE NOT FOUND_
```

What program sent the error message? ________________ At what level are you now? ________________ Can you enter a CP/M command now? ________________

- - - - - - - - - - - - - - - -

(a) CP/M searched for and loaded the COPY program, passed the operands to it, and gave it control; the COPY program ran and terminated and CP/M resumed control; (b) SORT, program level, no (you must have the CP/M prompt to enter a CP/M command)

CP/M CONTROL CHARACTERS

Whenever you're typing CP/M commands or using the CP/M built-in commands and transient programs, you can use a special set of control characters. In the next section of this chapter, you'll learn what these control characters are and how they make your console tasks much easier.

8. First, what is a control character? It's a keyboard character that you type while holding down the CONTROL key. Many of the keys on your terminal keyboard are capable of sending three different signals. If you hit the key without SHIFT, it sends the lower-case character, as a typewriter would. If you hold down the SHIFT key and hit a character key, it sends the upper-case character. If you hold down the CONTROL key and hit a character key, the control character is sent. Like the shift key, the CONTROL key doesn't do anything by itself.

Not all character keys on your keyboard have control values. On most terminals the letters do, but the numbers and symbols don't. If you hold down CONTROL and hit a non-control key, the result depends on your terminal. Our terminal sends the lower-case character.

CP/M displays a control character as two characters – a caret (^) followed by the upper-case letter for that key. So control-p is displayed this way: ^P. (Your terminal may display ^ as ↑.) We'll use this convention throughout this book, but it's important to remember that the control characters are one character, not two. The two keys are pressed at the same time, not one after the other.

(a) How do you type ^S? ________________

____

(b) If you press CONTROL by itself, what happens? ________________

- - - - - - - - - - - - - - - -

____

(a) hold down CONTROL and type the "s" key; (b) nothing

9. While you're typing a CP/M command, you may make a typing error. You can correct errors by using the control characters and the rubout or delete character.

Your terminal has a key labeled RUB or RUBOUT, or DEL or DELETE. This key erases the previous character from memory. CCP will echo the deleted character on your terminal display. For example, the key sequence E R R A (del) (del) A will produce this display:

ERRAARA_

Inside the system ERA will be stored.

If you type ARA XY and then notice that you meant to use ERA, you could enter six delete characters and start over. The corrected entry would look like this:

A>ARA XYYX ARAERA XY_

Only ERA XY is stored at this point and you can continue entering the filename.

(a) Suppose you intended to type SORT INVENTY.DAT and instead typed this:

SORT INVENTRY.DAT_

How many delete characters must you enter to correct it? ________

(b) How does the display appear after the delete characters are entered?

____

(c) What do you type to correct the entry now? ________

(d) What value is stored when you enter the corrected command?

____

- - - - - - - - - - - - - - - -

(a) 6; (b) SORT INVENTRY.DATTAD.YR; (c) Y.DAT; (d) SORT INVENTY.DAT

10. CP/M supplies several control codes that you can use to clean up your corrected displays and make them easier to read on the screen. Control-R (^R), control-U (^U), and control-H (^H) are all very useful when you are typing CP/M commands.

^R – this control character retypes the current command line, as it appears in memory, on a new console line. The echoed deleted characters will be removed. The key sequence E R R A (del) (del) A^R will produce this display:

ERRAARA#

ERA_

The pound sign (#) indicates that the old line has been abandoned. You can continue typing your command on the new line.

^U – this control character deletes the current command line from memory. On your terminal a pound sign is displayed and the cursor moves to the beginning of a new line. The key sequence ERRA^U would produce this display:

ERRA#

_

Newer versions of CP/M have some additional line correction commands:

^H – backspaces the cursor one position so that you can type over a letter. You could use ^H instead of rubout/delete. The key sequence E R R ^H A would produce this display:

ERA_

^X – backspaces the cursor to the beginning of the line. (In earlier versions, ^X is the same as ^U.)

(a) Examine this key sequence: S Q A (del) U A R E. What will be stored in memory? ________________

(b) If your command line gets hard to read, what character will display a "clean" version on a new line? ________________

(c) What character deletes the entire line? ________________

(d) On *your* system, what does ^X do?

______ a. Delete line (Skip question e.)

______ b. Backspaces cursor to beginning of line (Answer question e.)

(e) What character backspaces the cursor one character? ________________

- - - - - - - - - - - - - - - -

(a) SQUARE; (b) ^R; (c) ^U; (d) the answer depends on your system; (e) ^H

11. The ^C function is called the system reboot. When you type ^C, control is forced to the beginning of the CP/M program and parts of the system are read in from the disk in drive A. If that disk has been removed, you'll get an error message or the system will hang up.

You learned earlier that booting is also called a "cold start". Rebooting with a ^C is often called a "warm start".

^C can be used to stop a CP/M program when you don't want to continue. This is called "aborting" the program. ^C always returns you to the CP/M prompt, even from the program level. (A program that is not part of the CP/M system, such as a BASIC interpreter, may or may not recognize ^C; all CP/M programs do.)

(a) What is the effect of typing ^C while a CP/M system program is running?

___

(b) Does ^C cause the CP/M system to abort, cold start, or warm start?

___

(c) From where is the CP/M system read after ^C is entered? ___

___

- - - - - - - - - - - - - - - - -

(a) abort the program; (b) warm start; (c) the disk on drive A

12. When a CP/M program is executing, you can type ^C at any time to abort it. The program will respond to ^C within a few seconds.

However, when CCP is displaying the command prompt and waiting for input, ^C will only work at the beginning of the command line immediately after the prompt.

Suppose you have started to type a command and change your mind and decide to reboot. What commands do you need to type in order to reboot? Show them below.

```
A>SORT B:INV_
```

___

___

- - - - - - - - - - - - - - - - -

^U or ^X followed by A>^C

13. A cold start always puts you on A drive. A warm start leaves you on the active drive, even though it loads the system from drive A.

(a) Suppose you type:

```
A>^C
```

What will the system respond? ___

(b) Suppose you type:

```
B>^C
```

What will the system respond? ___

(c) Suppose you type:

```
A>ERA^C
```

What will the system respond? ___

___

(d) ^C is a fast way to return to the A drive from any other drive. True or false?

____

- - - - - - - - - - - - - - - -

(a) A>; (b) B>; (c) nothing – ^C must be the first character here to be recognized as a reboot; (d) false – ^C leaves you on the active drive

14. The ^S function interrupts system output until any other character is typed at the console. If a CP/M program is displaying a lot of data that is rolling off the top of your screen before you have a chance to read it, ^S will stop it. When you're ready to continue, hit any character except ^C. ^C will abort the program.

(a) Suppose you're displaying a file by using the built-in command TYPE. What character can you type to temporarily interrupt the display? ______________

(b) What character can you type to resume the display? ______________

(c) What character can you type to abort the TYPE function and return to command level? ______________

- - - - - - - - - - - - - - - -

(a) ^S; (b) any character except ^C; (c) ^C

15. If you're working at a video terminal and would like a hardcopy listing of your interactions with CP/M, ^P will turn on your line printer. The printer echoes each character you type and each character that CP/M displays. (Some printers store characters until you hit carriage return and will then print the whole line.) To turn off the echo print, simply hit ^P again. It acts like a toggle switch alternately turning the printer on and off.

(a) What character can you type to turn on the echo printing function? __________

(b) What character can you type to turn off the echo printing function? __________

- - - - - - - - - - - - - - - -

(a) ^P; (b) ^P

16. A cold or a warm start also turns off echo printing.

(a) What do you type to start echo printing? ______________

____

(b) Show three ways to turn off echo printing.

____

____

____

(c) Suppose you're using TYPE with echo printing on. You want to abort the program and continue working with echo printing on. Show the command, or commands, to abort a program and leave echo print on. ________________

____

- - - - - - - - - - - - - - - -

(a) ˆP; (b) ˆP, ˆC, boot; (c) ˆC followed by ˆP

17. All the CP/M programs recognize the ˆP command. Therefore you can turn echo printing on at the command level and execute a CP/M program. Echo printing will stay on throughout the program execution unless you turn it off or the program performs a reboot.

If you start executing a CP/M program without echo printing, you may or may not be able to turn echo printing on without returning to command level. Some of the CP/M programs, such as TYPE, are output-only programs. They are not expecting any input and therefore cannot recognize ˆP. To use echo printing with these programs, you must turn it on at the command level before you enter the CP/M command.

Other CP/M programs, such as ED, do recognize input. With these programs you can turn echo printing on and off at the program level.

Non-CP/M programs may not recognize ˆP. When you execute such a program, echo printing may get turned off automatically as soon as the program is started.

Match the programs described below with the statements on the right.

_____ (1) DIR is a built-in command that is output-only.

_____ (2) SORT is a non-CP/M program that allows input and output.

_____ (3) ED is a CP/M transient program that allows both input and output.

a. You can get a hardcopy of the output by turning on echo printing before entering the command.

b. You can get a hardcopy of part of the output by turning echo printing on and off while it is executing.

c. You can't get a hardcopy of the output using echo printing.

d. Any of the above may be correct because we don't know how the program works.

- - - - - - - - - - - - - - - -

(1) a; (2) d; (3) a, b

18. Recall that you can interrupt the output of a CP/M program with ^S. Recall also that *any other character,* except ^C, restarts the output.

Suppose you're typing a long file using the built-in command TYPE. After it starts, you decide you want to turn on echo printing. What can you do?

(a) Type ^C to abort the program, followed by ^P to turn on echo printing, then enter the TYPE command again.

(b) Type ^S to interrupt the output, followed by ^P to turn on echo printing, then ^S to restart the output.

(c) Nothing – you can't use echo printing with TYPE.

- - - - - - - - - - - - - - - -

a - (b is incorrect because the ^P would restart the output rather than turn on echo printing.)

19. All the control characters you have studied in this section – rubout/delete, ^R, ^X, ^U, ^H, ^C, ^S, and ^P – are CP/M control characters. They work when you are at CP/M command level. They may also work when you are at the program level, but that depends on the specific program.

If you are working with non-CP/M programs – programs that have been written or purchased elsewhere – you'll have to examine the program documentation to find out what control characters the program will recognize. Many programs that were written to work with CP/M will recognize the same characters, but others won't.

The CP/M built-in commands and transient programs recognize these control characters. Later on, as you study each program, we will remind you of the relevant control functions.

(a) The control characters are always recognized at the command level. True or false? ______________

(b) All CP/M programs recognize the control characters presented in this chapter. True or false? ______________

(c) All non-CP/M programs do not recognize the control characters presented in this chapter. True or false? ______________

- - - - - - - - - - - - - - - -

(a) true; (b) true; (c) false (some programs are written to recognize the same control characters)

20. There are basically two different ways for a program to handle input data. One way is to read each character, store it, and display it on the terminal screen but not process it until you hit the carriage return <CR> key. This is the most common way of handling input data that might contain more than one character, such as the CP/M commands. It gives you time to think, find the right keys, and correct typing errors before you hit <CR>.

The other way is to read a character and *process it immediately* (without waiting for you to push <CR>). This is sometimes used when the program is only expecting a one-letter command. For example, programs frequently ask yes or no questions such as:

DO YOU REALLY WANT TO QUIT (Y OR N)? _

The instant you type Y or N, it will be read and processed. This can be surprising if you're not expecting it; your display will change while you're still reaching for the <CR> key.

Some CP/M control characters (as mentioned previously) are processed immediately, even if typed in the middle of a command that's being stored. They're not stored as part of the command, and they're usually not displayed *per se.* (You see their *effect,* but the characters themselves are usually not displayed.)

What happens if you type another control character such as ^A? The effect depends on the specific character you type. There are some other CP/M control characters that we have not yet discussed – ^E, ^I, ^J, ^M, and ^Z. You'll learn about these in later chapters. Except for these, the system will treat a control character as a regular character: it is read, stored as part of the command, and displayed.

At the CP/M command level, identify whether the following characters would be stored or processed immediately.

(a) ^U ______________________________

(b) D ______________________________

(c) ^P ______________________________

(d) ^A ______________________________

(e) % ______________________________

(f) rubout/delete ______________________________

(g) ^C at the beginning of a line ______________________________

(h) ^C in the middle of a line ______________________________

- - - - - - - - - - - - - - - -

(a) processed; (b) stored; (c) processed; (d) stored; (e) stored; (f) processed; (g) processed; (h) stored

In this chapter you have studied the general CP/M command format, what happens when you enter a CP/M command, and the CP/M control characters. Now you're ready to begin learning the commands themselves, but first complete the Self-Test and try the machine exercises.

CHAPTER 2 SELF-TEST

This Self-Test will help you determine if you have mastered the objectives for this chapter. Answer each question to the best of your ability. Then check your answers in the answer key at the end of the test.

1. Assume that your disks contain these files:

Drive A	*Drive B*
PIP.COM	JOHNSON.LET
ED.COM	JONES.LET
TEST.COM	INDEX.PRN
TEST.DAT	INDEX.COM

(a) Write a command to run the ED program using the file JOHNSON.LET. Leave the A drive active.

A> ______________________________

(b) Write a command to run the INDEX program which requires no operands. Leave the A drive active.

A> ______________________________

(c) Rewrite your command for question (b) to leave the B drive active.

A> ______________________________

(d) Write a command to TYPE the file named INDEX.PRN. TYPE is a built-in command. Leave the B drive active.

B> ______________________________

(e) Write a command to TYPE the file named TEST.DAT. Leave the B drive active.

B> ______________________________

2. Suppose you had this CP/M interaction:

```
A>TYPE JONES.LET
FILE NOT FOUND

A>_
```

(a) What program issued the message FILE NOT FOUND? ______________

(b) What went wrong? ______________________________

____

(c) At what level are you now? ______________________________

(d) Can you enter a CP/M command now? ______________________

3. Suppose you had this CP/M interaction:

```
A>ERA TEST.DAT
A>_
```

(a) What happened? ______

(b) At what level are you now? ______

(c) Can you enter a CP/M command now? ______

4. Suppose you had this CP/M interaction:

```
A>INDEX
INDEX?

A>_
```

(a) What program issued the message INDEX? ______

(b) What went wrong? ______

______

(c) What level are you now at? ______

(d) Can you enter a CP/M command now? ______

5. The more you know about the control characters, the easier it will be for you to use your terminal. Give the correct character for each of the following functions. Try to work from memory.

(a) Restart CP/M from the beginning (system reboot; warm start; abort).

______

(b) Interrupt output display. ______

Restart output display. ______

(c) Echo print on. ______ Echo print off. ______

(d) Delete entire line. ______

(e) Delete previous letter. ______

(f) Reshow current line. ______

Only answer the following questions if your system includes these functions.

(g) Backspace one character. ______

(h) Backspace to beginning of line. ______

Chapter 2 Answer Key

Compare your answers to the Self-Test with the correct answers given below. If all your answers are correct, you are ready to go on to the next chapter. If you missed any questions you may find it helpful to review the appropriate frames before continuing.

1. (a) A>ED B:JOHNSON.LET; (b) A>B:INDEX; (c) A>B: followed by B>INDEX; (d) B>TYPE INDEX.PRN; (e) B>TYPE A:TEST.DAT

2. (a) TYPE; (b) JONES.LET is not on disk A; (c) command level; (d) yes

3. (a) TEST.DAT was erased; (b) command level; (c) yes

4. (a) CP/M; (b) INDEX.COM is not on disk A; (c) command level; (d) yes

5. (a) ^C; (b) ^S, any character but ^C; (c) ^P, ^P; (d) ^U and in some systems ^X; (e) rubout/delete; (f) ^R; (g) ^H; (h) ^X

Suggested Machine Exercises

Before you go on to the next chapter, you should practice some of the things you have learned here. You're not actually ready to enter any commands yet, but you can practice some of the control characters.

1. Start your system.
2. Boot.
3. When you've got the A prompt, continue.
4. Type this sentence: HI THERE.
5. Enter it. What response do you get? CCP should respond "HI?"
6. If you have a line printer, turn on echo print. (Do you remember how to do this? Hold down the CONTROL key and hit the letter P.) Type a few letters to make sure your printer is echoing. If not, hit carriage return. If it still doesn't print, check the following:
   (a) Is your printer cable connected?
   (b) Is your printer power on?
   (c) Is the printer on-line as opposed to local?
   (d) Did you hit ^P just once? Remember that it's a toggle switch. If none of the above succeeds, you may need to get some help from a colleague or your hardware/software dealer.

7. Reboot. (Use ^U or ^X to get to the beginning of a line to do this.)

8. Check echo printing; it should now be off. Turn it on again.

9. Type this sentence, but make a lot of mistakes and corrections:

   THE QUICK BROWN FOX JUMPS OVER THE LAZY DOG.

   Practice using delete/rubout; ^R if you need it, ^H and ^X if you have them. Compare your CRT display to the echo print listing.

10. Turn echo print off. Type a few letters to make sure it's off.

11. This is enough for now. Shut off the system and continue with Chapter 3.

CHAPTER THREE

CP/M Built-In Commands

CP/M has commands built into the Console Command Processor (CCP). These built-in commands will display all or part of a disk directory, display file contents, erase files, or change filenames. You can even create a file from whatever is in memory. CP/M version 2.0 allows you to change your user number as well. In this chapter, you'll see how to use the CP/M built-in commands to perform these functions.

When you complete your study of this chapter, you'll be able to:

- code specific (unambiguous) file references,
- code generalized (ambiguous) file references,
- display or print all or part of a disk directory,
- erase specified files from a disk,
- change the name of a file on a disk,
- display or print the contents of a (printable) file,
- create a file on disk from data in memory,
- assign or change a user number for CP/M version 2.0.

Versions 1.4 and earlier versions of CP/M support only one user. Later versions of CP/M support many users. When you first enter CP/M, you are in user area 0. If that doesn't change, you'll operate as a one-user system, as in basic CP/M. In this part of the chapter we'll consider user number 0 under version 2.0 to be equivalent in effect to version 1.4. Then we'll see how other user numbers are used and what effect they have on the built-in commands. You'll be able to skip over that section if your system is earlier than version 2.0.

THE DIR COMMAND

1. The DIR command is used to display the disk directory on the console. An entry like this:

```
A>DIR
```

results in a complete directory listing of the active disk at your console. If you want an echo print listing you can use ^P before entering DIR. Under Version 1.4, the directory is displayed as a list and looks like this:

```
A:PIP      COM
A:INVENTY  DAT
A:TEST     COB
A:SORT     COB
```

Under version 2.0, the directory looks like this:

```
A:PIP    COM:INVENTY    DAT:TEST    COB:SORT    COB
```

The entries are formatted four across and separated by colons. Column 1 contains the drivename in both versions. The period that separates the filename from the filetype is not included in either.

The directory listing of drive B can be obtained by entering DIR B:

Suppose drive C is active.

(a) How can you display its directory?

C> ______________________

(b) How can you display the directory on drive A?

C> ______________________

(c) What information is included in a directory listing?

____

- - - - - - - - - - - - - - -

(a) C>DIR; (b) C>DIR A: (or C>A:, A>DIR); (c) complete names of all files

2. The DIR command can be used to list a single file if you use the filename. If you specify A>DIR GAME.ONE, you will get one of two responses. If drive A contains a file named GAME.ONE, you'll get:

```
A:GAME   ONE
```

If drive A doesn't contain that file you'll get the message NOT FOUND.

Figure 3.1 contains a list of files that might appear on a disk. On this list, which commands below would result in the message NOT FOUND?

_____ (a) A>DIR COPY.COM

_____ (b) A>DIR TRY.NOW

_____ (c) A>DIR FIVE

_____ (d) A>DIR THREE.CH

- - - - - - - - - - - - - - -

b, c

(1)	TRY	(10)	PIP.COM	(19)	CORRES.XX
(2)	PRACTICE	(11)	ED.COM	(20)	CORRES.DK3
(3)	THIS.NOW	(12)	COPY.COM	(21)	BILLING.DT
(4)	ONE.CH	(13)	INVOICE.XX	(22)	SUPPLIES.DT
(5)	TWO.CH	(14)	INVOICE.WI	(23)	PROGRAM.COB
(6)	THREE.CH	(15)	INVOICE.DK	(24)	PROGRAM.REL
(7)	FOUR.CH	(16)	CORRES.WI	(25)	PROGRAM.PRN
(8)	FIVE.CH	(17)	CORRES.DK1	(26)	PROGRAM.DAT
(9)	INTRO.CH	(18)	CORR.DK2	(27)	PROGRAM.COM

Figure 3.1. File Listing, Drive A

3. Suppose you want to find out whether your B disk contains the INVENTY.DAT file. Which of the following commands would be the most efficient?

_____ (a) A>DIR B:

_____ (b) A>DIR B:INVENTY.DAT

_____ (c) A>DIR

- - - - - - - - - - - - - - - -

b

4. Like all of the built-in commands, DIR works very fast. If you're using a video terminal under version 1.4 and have a lot of files to be listed, some of the filenames may roll off the top of the screen before the listing is finished.

You can interrupt the listing with ^S. DIR works so fast that you may need to pose your fingers over the CONTROL and S keys *before* you enter the DIR command. (Echo printing slows down the output.)

DIR is an output-only function and is not expecting any input. If you type any character other than ^S while DIR is running, it will abort immediately.

(a) How can you temporarily stop the DIR listing? _______________

(b) How can you restart the listing again? _______________

(c) While the listing is stopped, how can you abort the DIR command? _______________

____

(d) While the listing is running, how can you abort the DIR command? _______________

____

- - - - - - - - - - - - - - - -

____

(a) type ^S; (b) type any character except ^C; (c) type ^C; (d) type any character except ^S

THE ERA COMMAND

5. The ERA built-in command is used to erase files from the directory and from the disk. Here is its format:

ERA file-name

The command ERA XYZ.PRN will erase the file of that name from the active disk directory. The space the file occupied is made available. The active drive prompt is displayed after the file is erased. If a file of that name doesn't exist on the active drive, the different versions have different responses. Version 2.0 and later versions return the message [NO FILE]. Older versions do not give you a message; therefore you won't know that nothing has been erased.

(a) Write a command to erase the first file from the list in Figure 3.1.

A> ____________________

(b) Suppose you have the following dialogue with CP/M:

```
A>ERA B:FERNANDEZ.LET
NO FILE
A>_
```

What happened? ____________________

____

(a) A>ERA TRY; (b) there is no file of that name on drive B

6. Files can be erased from any disk that is not read/only (R/O), if you prefix the filename with the drivename. ERA B:XYZ.COM will remove file XYZ.COM from the disk on drive B and from the directory of drive B. If you try to erase a file from a read/only disk, you get a BDOS error. Striking any key will reboot the system.

Write commands to accomplish the following functions.

(a) Erase the file named INVENTY.DAT from disk A. A> ____________

(b) Erase the file named COPY.COM from disk C. A> ____________

(c) Display the directory of disk C. A> ____________

(d) Display the directory of disk A. A> ____________

(e) Find out if COPY.COM is on disk B. A> ____________

____

____

(f) Erase COPY.COM from disk B. A> ______________________

(g) Check to see of COPY.COM was erased from disk B.

A> ______________________

- - - - - - - - - - - - - - - -

(a) A>ERA INVENTY.DAT; (b) A>ERA C:COPY.COM; (c) A>DIR C; (d) A>DIR; (e) A>DIR B:COPY.COM (or DIR B: but DIR B:COPY.COM is more efficient; (f) A>ERA B:COPY.COM; (g) A>DIR B:COPY.COM

THE REN COMMAND

7. The REN command is used to change the name of a file on a disk. REN just renames the file; it doesn't make another copy or move the file anywhere. REN is only concerned with the directory entry. Here is the format of the REN command:

REN new-name=old-name

Notice that the new name is specified first, followed by an equal sign and the filename as it currently exists. You may use spaces around the equal sign if you wish. The command REN NEW.ONE=XYZ.PRN will change the name of the current file XYZ.PRN on the active drive to NEW.ONE.

Write commands to change filenames on the active drive as indicated below:

(a) change ONE.CH to CHAP1.BK

____

(b) change PROGRAM.COM to PAYROLL.COM

____

(c) change PRACTICE to TRYOUT.DOC

____

- - - - - - - - - - - - - - - -

(a) REN CHAP1.BK=ONE.CH; (b) REN PAYROLL.COM=PROGRAM.COM; (c) REN TRYOUT.DOC=PRACTICE

8. Either or both of the filenames in the REN command can be preceded by a drivename. If you use a drivename on both filenames, they must be the same. If not, CP/M will question the second filename and won't rename anything. If you use a drivename on one filename, the same drive will be assumed for the other filename. If a drivename is not included, the active drive will be used.

Indicate which drive will be used for each valid REN command below. If the command is invalid give the reason.

(a) A>REN XYZ.PRN=XYZ.LST

____

(b) A>REN A:XYZ.PRN=XYZ.LST

____

(c) A>REN B:XYZ.PRN=A:XYZ.LST

____

(d) A>REN XYZ.PRN=B:XYZ.LST

____

(e) B>REN XYZ.PRN

____

\- - - - - - - - - - - - - - - -

(a) drive A; (b) drive A; (c) invalid, drivenames are different; (d) drive B; (e) invalid, only one filename is included

9. Aside from invalid REN commands, two types of errors may arise when you issue REN commands. You may name an old file that doesn't exist or you may give a new name that already does exist. In either case, no file is renamed. Suppose your disk contains these files:

```
FILE1.TEX     FILE1.BAK     TEX.COM
FILE2.TEX     FILE2.BAK     PIP.COM
FILE3.TEX     FILE3.BAK     ED.COM
```

You want to change FILE1.BAK to FILE1A.TEX. What happens if you code it like this?

```
REN FILE1.BAK=FILE1A.TEX
```

First the system looks for the old filename in the directory, but FILE1A.TEX doesn't exist and you will get an error message "NOT FOUND". Suppose you re-enter the line like this:

```
REN FILE2.TEX=FILE1.BAK
```

Now the system can locate FILE1.BAK in the directory to change it. It also checks the directory to be sure it isn't duplicating a filename. In this case, FILE2.TEX is in the directory and you get an error message "FILE EXISTS". If you really meant that last command, you would need to erase (ERA) or rename (REN) FILE2.TEX before renaming FILE1.BAK.

Refer once again to Figure 3.1. For each command below indicate the new filename or error message that results.

(a) A>REN CORRES.DK2=CORR.DK2

(b) A>REN A:TRY.OUT=TRY

(c) A>REN THREE.CH=THREE.CHP

(d) A>REN THREE.CH=PRACTICE

(e) A>REN A:FOUR.CHP=B:FOUR.CH

(f) A>REN PREFACE.CPM=INTRO.CH

- - - - - - - - - - - - - - - -

(a) new name of CORR.DK2 is CORRES.DK2; (b) new name of TRY is TRY.OUT; (c) message NOT FOUND; (d) message FILE EXISTS; (e) error – different drive-names (?B:FOUR.CH); (f) newname of INTRO.CH is PREFACE.CPM

10. Write commands to accomplish these operations on files from Figure 3.1.

(a) The INVOICE files are to be called BILL with the same filetypes.

(b) The PRACTICE file is to be named SIX.CH.

(c) BILLING.DT is to be changed to CORRES.WI. The old CORRES.WI can be removed.

- - - - - - - - - - - - - - - -

(a) REN BILL.XX=INVOICE.XX, REN BILL.WI=INVOICE.WI, REN BILL.DK=INVOICE.DK; (b) REN SIX.CH=PRACTICE; (c) ERA CORRES.WI, REN CORRES.WI=BILLING.DT

THE TYPE COMMAND

11. The TYPE built-in command displays the contents of a file at the console. Here is the TYPE format:

TYPE filename

As with other commands, a drivename can precede the filename. The file must contain printable characters such as textual material, source coding, or character data. Files of non-printable characters such as COM files, will try to type, but you'll see garbage on the screen. (If your terminal has a bell, it may also ring several times. This won't hurt the terminal.)

(a) How can you use TYPE to produce a printed copy of a file on the line printer?

____

(b) How can you temporarily stop a partially displayed file? ________________

(c) How can you restart it? ________________________________

(d) How can you permanently stop (abort) a file that is typing at the console?

____

\- - - - - - - - - - - - - - - -

(a) use ^P before carriage return; (b) use ^S; (c) type any character but ^C; (d) hit any key other than ^S

12. Refer to Figure 3.1 again. Suppose your A drive is active and you enter this command:

TYPE THIS.NEW

The system will respond with ?THIS.NEW – it couldn't find a file with that name. If you enter TYPETHIS.NOW, the system will respond ?TYPETHIS.NOW – you left out the space and the CCP didn't recognize TYPE. If you enter TYPE THIS.NOW, the contents of that file will be displayed on the screen (if it's printable).

Write commands to display the contents of the files from Figure 3.1. Assume drive B is active.

(a) file (23)

B> ____________________________________

(b) file (2)

B> ______________________________

(c) file (10)

B> ______________________________

(d) The COM file isn't in printable form. How can you cancel the display?

____

- - - - - - - - - - - - - - - -

(a) B>TYPE A:PROGRAM.COB; (b) B>TYPE A:PRACTICE;
(c) B>TYPE A:PIP.COM; (d) hit any key (except ^S)

13. Refer to Figure 3.1 and write commands to perform the sequence of operations below.

(a) Display a complete directory.

A> ______________________________

(b) Remove the PROGRAM file of type PRN.

A> ______________________________

(c) Change the name of the REL type PROGRAM file to PATCH.REL.

A> ______________________________

(d) Display the contents of the PROGRAM file of type COB.

A> ______________________________

(e) Produce a printed listing of PROGRAM.COB.

A> ______________________________

(f) Stop the display of PROGRAM.COB in mid-TYPE.

____

- - - - - - - - - - - - - - - -

(a) A>DIR; (b) A>ERA PROGRAM.PRN; (c) REN PATCH.REL=PROGRAM.REL;
(d) A>TYPE PROGRAM.COB; (e) use ^P before the TYPE command is entered;
(f) use ^S at the appropriate time

THE SAVE COMMAND

14. The SAVE built-in command is used to put the contents of the Transient Program Area (TPA) on disk as a file. This is the SAVE command format:

SAVE n filename

Here *n* refers to the number of "pages" of data – CP/M considers 256 bytes to be a page. You'll use the SAVE command only if you're involved with assembler language programming or regenerating a system. But since it is a built-in command, we're introducing SAVE here.

SAVE 3 FILE.XY

This example causes the first three pages (three x 256 bytes) in the TPA to be written on the active disk and named FILE.XY. Just as you can't ERAse or REName a file on a Read/Only disk, you can't SAVE a file onto an R/O disk.

Which of these SAVE commands is in correct format?

_____ (a) SAVE PROGRAM.COM

_____ (b) SAVE 6 ZAP.COM

_____ (c) SAVE ZAP.COM 6

_____ (d) SAVE6ZAP.COM

- - - - - - - - - - - - - - - -

b

GENERALIZED FILE REFERENCES

15. A file reference is used to identify a particular file or group of files on a disk. The file reference is specific when it refers to a single file; CP/M documentation calls this an "unambiguous filename" or "ufn." Any file reference that includes the drive, the filename, and the filetype refers to only one file and is unambiguous. The drive can be omitted if the appropriate disk is on the active drive.

A generalized file reference may refer to a number of different files. CP/M calls this an "ambiguous filename" or "afn." One way of specifying a generalized file reference is to use an asterisk for either the filename or filetype, and the actual filename or filetype for the other. *.COM refer to all the files on the active disk that have filetype "COM," no matter what the specific file name is.

Label the file references below as specific or generalized.

(a) B:INVENT.DEC _______________

(b) INVENT.* _______________

(c) A:*.DEC _______________

(d) INVENT.DEC ______________________________

(e) Which of the file references above are unambiguous (ufn)?

____

(f) Which of the file references above could refer to more than one file?

____

- - - - - - - - - - - - - - - -

(a) specific; (b) generalized; (c) generalized; (d) specific; (e) a, d; (f) b, c

16. A complete file reference may include a drivename as well as a filename and filetype. Either the filename or the filetype, or both, can be replaced with an asterisk. The asterisk means that any combination of characters will do. The drivename cannot be replaced with an asterisk since a command can deal with only one disk drive at a time. However, the drivename can be omitted if the active drive is appropriate. Match the file references with their descriptions.

______ (a)	*.PRN	(1) Invalid file reference.
______ (b)	JOBTIME.*	(2) Refers to all files with filetype PRN.
______ (c)	*:JOBTIME.PRN	(3) Refers to all files with filename JOBTIME
______ (d)	*:*.*	(4) Refers to all files on all disk drives.
______ (e)	*.*	(5) Refers to all files on the active disk.
______ (f)	B:*.COM	(6) Refers to all files with filetype COM.
		(7) None of these.

- - - - - - - - - - - - - - - -

(a) 2; (b) 3; (c) 1; (d) 1; (e) 5; (f) 7

17. Suppose the active disk contains these files:

PAYROLL.COB	PIP.COM
PAYROLL.REL	ED.COM
PAYROLL.PRN	COPY.COM
PAYROLL.DAT	DISKTST.COM

Write file references that refer to the files described below.

(a) All the files that have PAYROLL as the basic filename.

____

____

(b) All the files that have filetype COM.

____

(c) The COBOL source file (type COB) for the PAYROLL program.

____

(d) All the files on the disk.

____

- - - - - - - - - - - - - - - -

(a) PAYROLL.*; (b) *.COM; (c) PAYROLL.COB; (d) *.*

18. You have seen how the asterisk is used to indicate a generalized file name. The asterisk indicates *any number* of ambiguous characters – up to eight for the filename or three for the filetype.

You can also use a question mark (?) as a character in an ambiguous filename. The question mark indicates just *one* ambiguous character. The reference ?TEST.DAT would be matched with any of these filenames: ATEST.DAT, BTEST.DAT, CTEST.DAT, etc. But it would not be matched by NEWTEST.DAT or A1TEST.DAT.

To answer the questions below, assume that your active disk contains these files:

PAYROLLS.COM
PAYROLL1.DAT
PAYROLL2.DAT
PAYTAXES.COM
PAYTAXES.DAT
PAYROLLS.COB
PAYTAXES.COB

(a) Name any files that match PAYROLL?.DAT

____

(b) Name any files that match PAY?????.COM.

____

(c) Name any files that match PAYTAXES.CO?

____

- - - - - - - - - - - - - - - -

(a) PAYROLL1.DAT and PAYROLL2.DAT; (b) PAYROLLS.COM and PAYTAXES.COM; (c) PAYTAXES.COM and PAYTAXES.COB

19. The question mark can be used to set any position in a filename or filetype, to refer to any character. The reference X?Z.* refers to any three character filename that begins with X and ends with Z, no matter what the filetype is. These files are all included.

XYZ
XYZ.TEM
X2Z.PRN
XAZ.B

Suppose a disk contains these files:

D330T1.WS
D330B1.WS
D330C1.WS
D331T1.WST
D331B1.WST
D330C1.TWS
PIP.COM
WS.COM

Write file references to refer to the groups of files indicated below.

(a) All the files whose filename ends with T1.

____

(b) All the files whose filename includes 330.

____

(c) All the files of filetype WS and filename ending with C1.

____

- - - - - - - - - - - - - - - -

(a) D33?T1.* or ????T1.*; (b) ?330??.*; (c) ????C1.WS

20. Under CP/M the filename has eight characters while the filetype has three characters. A blank is considered a specific character. The filename PIP.COM is really PIPb̸b̸b̸b̸b̸.COM, where b̸ indicates a blank. The filename TESTDATA is really TESTDATA.b̸b̸b̸.

If you use the generalized reference P?.COM, you have really specified P?b̸b̸b̸b̸b̸b̸.COM. A matching filename will have blanks in positions 3 through 8; that is, it must be no more than two characters long. These filenames would match: P1.COM, PT.COM, and P.COM. But the filenames PIP.COM and PAYROLLS.COM would not match.

Suppose a disk contains these files:

XYZ.A	XYZ	X006.A
XYY.A	XYX	X007.A
XYY.B	WALL	X008.B
XYX.B	ROOM	X009.C

Which files are included by each file reference below.

(a) ???.* ______

(b) ??X.* ______

(c) * ______

(d) X???????.A ______

(e) X???.B ______

(f) X??.B ______

- - - - - - - - - - - - - - - - -

(a) XYZ.A, XYY.A, XYY.B, XYX.B, XYZ, XYX; (b) XYX.B, XYX; (c) XYZ, XYX, WALL, ROOM; (d) XYZ.A, XYY.A, X006.A, X007.A; (e) XYY.B, XYX.B, X008.B; (f) XYY.B, XYX.B

21. In writing generalized file references the asterisk is really an abbreviation that fills the rest of a filename or filetype field with question marks. Examine these examples:

TE*.PRN	is equivalent to TE??????.PRN
TE*.*	is equivalent to TE??????.???

Characters following an asterisk are ignored. *EE.COM is equivalent to *.COM or ????????.COM. The asterisk causes the field it appears in to be filled with question marks. This will create the generalized (ambiguous) file reference.

The files in figure 3.1 are numbered for your convenience. Indicate which files match each file reference below.

(a) * ______

(b) T??.* ______

(c) T*.CH ______

(d) C*.* ______

(e) C*.D* ______

(f) *.WI ______

(g) *ES.D* ______

(h) P*.C* ____________________

(i) P* ____________________

- - - - - - - - - - - - - - - -

(a) 1, 2; (b) 1, 5; (c) 5, 6; (d) 12, 16, 17, 18, 19, 20; (e) 17, 18, 20; (f) 14, 16; (g) 15, 17, 18, 20, 21, 22, 26 (don't forget that the characters following * will be ignored); (h) 10, 23, 27; (i) 2

Now that you've learned how to write a generalized file reference, let's practice some DIR and ERA commands. SAVE, TYPE, and REN must have specific filenames.

22. In the DIR command the filename can be specific or generalized, as in these examples:

B:	This refers to all files on drive B.
.	This refers to all files on the active drive.
X??.*	This is a typical generalized file reference.
XYZ.COM	This refers to a specific file.

Write two different commands to display the complete directory on the active drive.

(a) ____________________

(b) ____________________

What is the general effect of each DIR command below?

(c) DIR * ____________________

____

(d) DIR *.* ____________________

____

(e) DIR *.COM ____________________

____

(f) DIR T*.PRN ____________________

____

(g) DIR T?6?.PRN ____________________

____

- - - - - - - - - - - - - - - -

(a) DIR; (b) DIR *.*; (c) list all files on the active drive with no (or blank) filetype; (d) list entire directory (all files) on the active drive; (e) list all COM files (filetype COM) on the active drive; (f) list all PRN files with filename beginning with T on the active drive; (g) list all PRN files on the active drive that have filenames of three or four characters with T in the first position and 6 in the third

23. Refer to Figure 3.1. Assume drive A is active. Which of the DIR commands below will return the NOT FOUND message?

_____ (a) DIR CORRE.*

_____ (b) DIR PRACTICE.*

_____ (c) DIR PROGRAM

_____ (d) DIR *.CH?

_____ (e) DIR IN??.*

_____ (f) DIR IN*.*

_____ (g) DIR XYZ.COM

- - - - - - - - - - - - - - - - -

(a) (No filename is CORRE.); (c) (no PROGRAM filename has a blank filetype); (e) (No filename starting with IN has only four characters); (g) (No file with that name is on the disk.)

24. Use Figure 3.1 and give the numbers of filenames that would be included in directory listings produced by these DIR commands.

(a) DIR PRACTICE.* _____

(b) DIR *.CH? _____

(c) DIR IN*.* _____

(d) DIR CO???.* _____

(e) DIR P*.* _____

(f) DIR ??V*.* _____

- - - - - - - - - - - - - - - - -

(a) 2; (b) 4, 5, 6, 7, 8, 9; (c) 9, 13, 14, 15; (d) 12, 18; (e) 2, 10, 23, 24, 25, 26, 27; (f) 8, 13, 14, 15

25. The ERA command can also reference a generalized filename. Refer again to Figure 3.1. How many files are removed from the disk by each ERA command below?

(a) ERA PRACTICE ____________________

(b) ERA PROGRAM.* ____________________

(c) ERA CORRES.DK2 ____________________

(d) ERA *.COM ____________________

(e) ERA F*.CH ____________________

(f) ERA T??.CH ____________________

(g) ERA XYZ.COM ____________________

(h) ERA BILLING.DT ____________________

(i) ERA * ____________________

- - - - - - - - - - - - - - - -

(a) 1; (b) 5; (c) none; (d) 4; (e) 2; (f) 1; (g) none; (h) 1; (i) 2

26. All files can be erased from a disk with the command ERA *.*. When you enter this command CP/M gives you the message "ALL FILES (Y/N)?". If you enter "Y," all files on the disk are erased. If you enter "N," the ERA *.* command is canceled and nothing is erased.

Suppose you have disks on drives A and B that contain these files:

drive A	drive B
PROGRAM.COB	TRY
PROGRAM.REL	PRACTICE
PROGRAM.PRN	THIS.NOW
PROGRAM.DAT	INVOICE.XX
PROGRAM.COM	INVOICE.DK
PIP.COM	INVOICE.WI
ED.COM	

Write commands to accomplish the following functions, working from the active drive indicated.

(a) Remove PIP.COM from disk A.

A> ____________________

(b) Display the complete directory of the disk on drive B.

A> ____________________

(c) Remove files TRY and PRACTICE from drive B.

A> ____________________

(d) Change the active drive to B.

A> ________________________________

(e) Remove all the PROGRAM files from drive A.

B> ________________________________

(f) Remove the INVOICE files from drive B.

B> ________________________________

(g) Display the directory listing for drive A.

B> ________________________________

(h) Sketch the resulting display.

____

____

____

- - - - - - - - - - - - - - - - -

(a) A>ERA PIP.COM
(b) A>DIR B:
(c) A>ERA B:*
(d) A>B:
(e) B>ERA A:PROGRAM.*
(f) B>ERA INVOICE.*
(g) B>DIR A:
(h) A:ED COM

27. Refer to Figure 3.1. Assume drive A is active. Write commands to erase files as indicated below.

(a) Remove files (4) through (9).

____

(b) Remove all the files.

____

(c) Remove files (16) through (20).

____

- - - - - - - - - - - - - - - - -

(a) ERA *.CH; (b) ERA *.*; (c) ERA COR*.* (or COR???.* or CORR*.*)

VERSION 2.0 ENHANCEMENTS

You've seen how the CP/M built-in commands are used in version 1.4 and single user (0) version 2.0. DIR, ERA, RENAME, and TYPE have some differences in version 2.0. In addition, version 2.0 has a new built-in command, USER. If you use version 1.4 or earlier, you may skip ahead to the Self-Test if you wish.

USER NUMBERS

28. Version 2.0 allows 16 different user numbers (0-15). Internally, user numbers are associated with files. If you create a file as user 5, for example, that file is associated with user number 5. Other user numbers can not access the file. After a cold start the system puts you in user number 0. If you don't change that, you'll operate just as you learned for version 1.4. If you do change the user number, CP/M moves to another part of the directory. Files associated with user 0 can no longer be accessed, although the active drive remains the same. The user number remains the same until you change it or until another cold start is performed.

(a) How many user numbers does version 2.0 support? ____________________

(b) What user number is in effect directly after a cold start? ________________

(c) Suppose a disk contains files attached to user numbers 0, 1, 2 and 6. Can you access all the files at any given time? ______________________________

____

- - - - - - - - - - - - - - - - -

(a) 16; (b) 0; (c) no – only those for the active user number

29. The USER built-in command is used to change user numbers. Here is its format:

USER n

For example, USER 5 selects user number 5. The n can be a number from 0 through 15. The selected user number remains in effect until another USER command is issued or a cold start is performed.

How would you accomplish the following:

(a) Select user number 0.

____

(b) Select user number 11.

____

____

(c) Select user number 2.

____

- - - - - - - - - - - - - - - -

(a) cold start or USER 0; (b) USER 11; (c) USER 2

30. Under version 2.0, a user number is associated with each directory entry. When you enter DIR you get a directory listing of all files associated with the active user number. Of course, if all files are associated with the same user number, you'll get a complete listing.

(a) Explain why a 2.0 DIR listing might not include all the files on the disk.

____

____

(b) Suppose you are under USER 0 and you want directory listings of all files associated with user numbers 0 and 5. Write the commands you need.

____

____

____

____

- - - - - - - - - - - - - - - -

(a) Only the non-system files of the active user are listed;
(b) DIR; USER 5; DIR

31. The ERA, REN, and TYPE commands can refer only to files associated with the active user. If you enter ERA *.*, you will erase all files associated with the current user number. If you attempt to rename a file that has a different user number, you'll get a NOT FOUND message. If you try to erase a file that has a different user number, the result will be the same as if the file didn't exist. If you try to TYPE a file that isn't attached to the active user number, it won't be typed – just questioned as a nonexistent file. The point is that CP/M can only recognize filenames attached to the current user number. You can perform the desired operation by changing to the correct user number. In later chapters you'll learn more about handling files and determining user numbers on a disk.

(a) How many commands are needed to erase all user files from a disk that has user numbers 2,3, and 4? Assume you have just done a cold start.

____

____

(b) How could you rename a file of user 7 if user 6 is active?

____

\- - - - - - - - - - - - - - - -

(a) 6 (3 USER commands and 3 ERA *.* commands); (b) change to USER 7 and use the REName command

32. The SAVE command also has a slightly different effect under version 2.0, but for a different reason. When you SAVE a file the active user number becomes associated with it. In version 1.4 the memory area in the TPA is likely to be destroyed by the SAVE operation, so a file can only be SAVEd once. In version 2.0 the TPA isn't altered by SAVE, so the same set of "pages" can be SAVEd under several different filenames and user numbers.

(a) Under what user number is a file SAVEd? ________________________

(b) Suppose you have a six "page" program in the TPA under user number seven. Write the commands to create two files, one called SAVONE.COM attached to user seven, and one called SAVTWO.COM attached to user eight.

____

____

____

\- - - - - - - - - - - - - - - -

(a) the active user; (b) SAVE 6 SAVONE.COM, USER 8, SAVE 6 SAVTWO.COM

As you've seen, user numbers supported under CP/M version 2.0 affect most of the built-in commands. The DIR command lists only files associated with the active user. ERA allows you to erase only files of the active user. REN lets you rename only files of the active user. And only those files can be TYPEd as well. The SAVE command allows you to resave the same area of the TPA. USER, a sixth built-in command, allows you to move freely between the various user areas on a disk. As you continue in your study of CP/M, you'll see many applications for these features of built-in commands under CP/M version 2.0.

(1)	PIP.COM	(8)	SUPPLY.FIL	(15)	SALES.DOC
(2)	ED.COM	(9)	COPY.DOC	(16)	SALES.HST
(3)	COPY.COM	(10)	SUPPLY.DOC	(17)	SALES.FIL
(4)	SUPPLY.ASM	(11)	RECORDS.LOC	(18)	ST.LST
(5)	SUPPLY.REL	(12)	RECORDS.STT	(19)	ST.DOC
(6)	SUPPLY.PRN	(13)	RECORD.ORD	(20)	DISK.DOC
(7)	SUPPLY.COM	(14)	RECL.AV		

Figure 3.2. Files on Drive B

CHAPTER 3 SELF-TEST

This Self-Test will help you determine if you have mastered the objectives of this chapter. Answer each question to the best of your ability. Then check your answers in the answer key at the end of the test.

These questions are based on the disk containing the files shown in Figure 3.2. We will use version 1.4 CP/M, or version 2.0 with only user 0 on the system, for the first nine questions.

1. Write commands to display the entire directory.

   A> ____

2. Write a command to display all directory entries with filenames beginning with S, no matter what the filetype is.

   B> ____

3. Write a command to remove all DOC type files from drive B.

   B> ____

4. Write a command to change the name of RECL.AV to REC.ASM.

   B> ____

5. Write a command to display the contents of file SUPPLY.FIL on the console.

   B> ____

6. Suppose SUPPLY.FIL contains about 200 lines of data. How can you read the first few lines at your console?

   ____

7. How can you produce a printed copy of SUPPLY.FIL on the line printer?

   ____

   ____

8. Write a command to create a file named "MEM.SAV" from eight "pages" in the TPA. Store MEM.SAV on drive A.

   B> ____

9. Consider the files shown in Figure 3.2. Suppose you have just cold started the system. You have several things to do.

   - Erase files (11), (12), and (13).
   - Type printed copies of files (15) and (17).
   - Change the name of file (18) to STATES.
   - Change the name of SUPPLY.FIL to be INVENTY.DAT.
   - Examine the complete directory listing at the console.

   Write all the commands you would need. Show the prompt at the beginning of each line to indicate the active drive.

   A>

The next three questions relate only to CP/M version 2.0 with multiple user numbers.

10. Give two ways you can access user number zero.

    ____

    ____

11. Suppose you are using a disk on which files are associated with user numbers 0, 3, and 7. How can you examine all the user directory entries?

    ____

    ____

12. Suppose you are using the same disk as above (11) and have just cold started the system. Write these commands:

    (a) Remove OPENST.REC from user 3.

    (b) Rename user 7 file OUTGO.BK to be called CASHFLOW.OUT.

    (c) Display the contents of user 0 file DIRECT.ION.

Chapter 3 Answer Key

Compare your answers to the Self-Test with the correct answers given below. If all your answers are correct you are ready to go on to the next chapter. If you missed any questions, you may find it helpful to review the appropriate frames from this chapter.

1. DIR B: or DIR B:*.*. Alternatively, you could switch drives then issue DIR.

2. DIR S*.* or DIR S?????.*

3. ERA *.DOC or ERA ????????.DOC

4. REN REC.ASM=RECL.AV

5. TYPE SUPPLY.FIL

6. Type ^S as soon as several lines appear on the console.

7. Type ^P before entering the TYPE command.

8. SAVE 8 A:MEM.SAV

9.
```
A>B:                              (If you omitted this step, your file references
                                  all need the drive prefix)
B>ERA RECO*.*                     (R*.* or REC*.* will also erase file (14) )
B>TYPE SALES.DOC                  (Enter ^P first)
B>TYPE SALES.FIL                  (Enter ^P after)
B>REN STATES=ST.LST
B>REN INVENTY.DAT=SUPPLY.FIL
B>DIR                             (or DIR *.* – You may need to use ^S)
```

10. cold start CP/M or USER 0

11. You will need to use three DIR commands and change user numbers between them.

12. (a) USER 3; ERA OPENST.REC
    (b) USER 7; REN CASHFLOW.OUT=OUTGO.BK
    (c) USER 0; TYPE DIRECT.ION

Machine Exercise Suggestions

If you have a CP/M system available, you may want to spend some time getting used to the built-in commands before you continue. The following machine practice will help.

1. Start up system and boot. (Use a copy of your original CP/M disk.)
2. Install another disk in drive B.
3. Get a directory of A disk.
4. Get a directory of B disk.
5. If you have a line printer, turn on echo printing and get a directory of A disk. Notice how much slower the output is. Turn off echo printing.
6. Get another directory of A, and this time interrupt the display and start again.
7. Rename PIP.COM as COPY.COM. (If your disk already has a COPY.COM, rename PIP.COM as PIP2.COM.)
8. Check the directory for all COM files. PIP.COM should not appear but your new name should.
9. Change the file with a new name – PIP2.COM or COPY.COM – back to PIP.COM again and recheck the directory.
10. Save 2 pages of the TPA as PRACTICE.PRN. (Don't worry about what you're saving. Some nonsense data will get saved.)

11. Display the directory. PRACTICE.PRN should appear.
12. Type PRACTICE.PRN. A couple of lines of meaningless data should be displayed.
13. Erase PRACTICE.PRN and recheck the directory.

The remaining steps pertain to user numbers under version 2.0. If you are working with an earlier version of CP/M, skip the remaining steps and go on to Chapter 4.

14. Change to user 2.
15. Check your directory. Are there any files for user 2?
16. Save two pages of the TPA as PRACTICE.PRN.
17. Check the directory again. PRACTICE.PRN should appear.
18. Go back to user 0 and check the directory. PRACTICE.PRN should not appear.
19. As user 0, try to type PRACTICE.PRN. You should get an error message.
20. As user 0, try to erase PRACTICE.PRN. Do you get a message?
21. Go back to user 2 and erase PRACTICE.PRN. Check the directory. Is it gone?

This completes the suggested machine exercises for Chapter 3. Shut down your system and go on to Chapter 4.

CHAPTER FOUR

CP/M Transient Programs

The typical 8-inch CP/M system disk contains the system on tracks 0 and 1. The commands you learned to use in the last chapter are built into the console command processor of CP/M. The disk also contains various transient programs that are supplied by Digital Research or your supplier. These transient programs can be used to get information about your disks, to perform common operations, to create files, and to assemble or compile new programs.

In this chapter we're going to overview the transient programs routinely supplied by Digital Research as a part of the CP/M system disk. You probably won't use all of these, but it's a good idea to know what's available. As you use CP/M on the job, you'll quickly learn which of these transient programs you'll need to use a great deal.

When you complete this chapter, you will be able to:

- Differentiate between built-in and transient programs.
- Identify the CP/M transient programs that would be used to perform various functions.
- Use the DUMP transient program to produce a listing in hexadecimal format of any file.
- Use the SYSGEN transient program to copy the CP/M system tracks to another disk.
- Use the MOVCPM transient program to place the CP/M system tracks in memory or change the system size.

1. In the last chapter you learned to use the CP/M built-in commands. These are built into the CP/M system and are included in the system tracks on a disk. Whenever CP/M is running, those built-in commands are present and can be used. Now we're going to look at CP/M's transient programs. These are programs provided by Digital Research in addition to the CP/M system itself. They aren't included on the system tracks, so a given CP/M disk might not include all of these. However, your master disk will have them. You'll eventually want to copy the transient programs you use on a regular basis, onto many of your disks.

(a) How are built-in programs different from transient programs, in terms of where they are located on a disk?

____

____

(b) Which type of CP/M programs are automatically "on" any CP/M disk?

____

(c) What type of CP/M program might *not* be included on every initialized CP/M disk?

____

- - - - - - - - - - - - - - - -

(a) built-in programs are on system tracks, transient programs are on other tracks; (b) built-in; (c) transient

2. The transient programs provided with CP/M serve several purposes. We'll overview all of them in this chapter. Later chapters are devoted to a more detailed study of some of the major CP/M transients.

Each CP/M transient program is on the disk in the form of a file of filetype COM – also called a COM file. They can be run by entering the filename (without COM) and any required parameters. You'll learn what parameters are required for each. Here is a directory listing of a CP/M disk that contains only the standard CP/M transient programs:

```
A:ASM          COM
A:LOAD         COM
A:DDT          COM
A:SYSGEN       COM
A:MOVCPM       COM
A:DUMP         COM
A:STAT         COM
A:PIP          COM
A:ED           COM
A:SUBMIT       COM
```

Which of the programs below can be run from this disk:

______ (a) SAVE

______ (b) SUBGEN

______ (c) PIP

______ (d) REN

______ (e) SYSGEN

______ (f) ED

- - - - - - - - - - - - - - - -

a, c, d, e, f (a and d are built-in and available on every CP/M disk. b – SUBGEN – is not on the disk.)

3. The ED program is CP/M's text editor. You use it to make new files or change old ones. ED is concerned with "ASCII" files, made up of strings of characters. Typical ASCII files might be correspondence, a chapter in a book, a mailing list, or a source program written in any language supported by the computer.

To use ED you enter a command in this format:

ED specific-file-name [destination drive]

If the file you specify exists, ED will let you change it or add to it. If the file doesn't exist, ED will create a directory entry and let you put information in the file. You can determine what filetype to use by the kind of data the file can provide. For example, an assembler program file must have type ASM. Other programs require such types as COB (COBOL), FOR (Fortran), or PLM (PL/M). Most other files may have whatever filetype seems appropriate. One very common filetype used for textual files is TEX. We'll cover ED in detail later in this book. [destination drive] is an optional drive name of form B:. This tells ED to put the edited file out to a specific disk. It leaves the current file where it is.

Suppose a disk contains only these files: ED.COM, PROG1.ASM, and PROG1.TEX.

(a) What can you do with PROG1.TEX after you enter the command shown below?

A>ED PROG1.TEX

(b) What command will let you create a file called TWO.COM?

(c) What command will let you modify the assembler language source program?

(a) change it or add to it; (b) ED TWO.COM; (c) ED PROG1.ASM

4. The PIP program (PIP.COM) is CP/M's file handling utility program. With PIP (it stands for peripheral interchange program) you can copy files from one disk to another or from a disk to any peripheral device. In fact PIP does all the internal conversions needed to load, print, punch, copy, and combine disk files. What you can do with PIP is limited only by the peripheral devices of your system. We'll devote an entire chapter to PIP later in the book.

PIP is used to transfer files from a disk to any device. When you want a transient program to be copied to a new disk, you need to PIP it over. Any file, of any filetype, can be PIPped. Under version 2.0, you can PIP a file from any user area to the active user area. You may find you want the PIP transient program on every CP/M disk you use. PIP can also be used to make another copy of a file on the same disk – under a different name.

(a) Which of these can be copied to another disk with PIP?

_____ ED.COM

_____ ERA

(b) Which of these transfers can be performed using PIP?

_____ disk-to-disk

_____ printer-to-disk

_____ disk-to-printer

- - - - - - - - - - - - - - - -

(a) ED.COM; (b) disk-to-disk or disk-to-printer

5. The STAT transient program provides general status information about a disk, a user number, or a file. STAT tells you the size of a file and whether it is read/only or read/write. It tells how much space is left on a disk or how many (and which) user numbers are active on the disk. You can also use STAT to change the file status. You'll learn to do this in the next chapter.

The SUBMIT transient program lets you use a single command to refer to a set of CP/M commands. To use SUBMIT you must first create a file of type SUB using the ED program. This SUB file contains other CP/M commands and parameters. It may include XSUB, another CP/M transient program referenced only from within SUB files. As you'll see, several operations take a number of different commands and parameters. You'll learn in the final chapter to create your own files for submitting to CP/M.

(a) What program provides status information about files or disks?

____

(b) What program lets you execute a series of CP/M commands by entering a single command? ______________________________________

(c) What program is used to create a new file? ____________________

- - - - - - - - - - - - - - - -

(a) STAT; (b) SUBMIT; (c) ED

6. Identify the CP/M transient program that would be used to accomplish each function below:

(a) Copy a file from one disk to another ____________________

____

(b) Copy a file from one disk to another, erase the original file and list the directory of the source disk – with a single command. ______________

(c) Identify the user numbers active on a particular disk. ______________

(d) Modify the contents of a TEX file ______________

– – – – – – – – – – – – – – – –

(a) PIP.COM; (b) SUBMIT.COM; (c) STAT.COM: (d) ED.COM

PROGRAM-RELATED TRANSIENTS

Three of the CP/M transient programs are closely related to programming your microcomputer. We're not going to teach you to write assembler language programs in this book. However, we will show you how to use the ASM, LOAD, and DDT commands to invoke these transient programs. You'll also learn what is needed as input and produced as output for each.

7. The ASM program is one of the CP/M assemblers. It translates a source file written in 8080 Assembler Language into your machine's internal language – the only language that your computer can understand.

If you are going to program your computer using Assembler Language, this is what you would do. Use ED to create a source file of Assembler Language commands. Your filetype will be ASM; for example, you might create a file named PAY7.ASM.

Then use the ASM program to *translate* the file into machine language. ASM takes a file of type ASM, "assembles" it, and produces two output files. Both output files have the same filename as the ASM file, but one has filetype HEX while the other has filetype PRN.

The HEX file contains the hexadecimal number system form of your machine language code. This is printable, but not very readable. The PRN file contains a copy of your original source file with the hexadecimal equivalent of each line, along with any error messages. The PRN file is somewhat readable. By displaying the PRN file, you can find out how your source code was translated and also what errors were identified by the ASM program.

Suppose your disk contains these files: ASM.COM, LOAD.COM, PAY7.ASM, MAIL.ASM and MAIL.DAT. A command like this will assemble the PAY7 program:

```
A>ASM PAY7
```

The filetype isn't entered, although it must be ASM. This command invokes the CP/M assembler and produces as output PAY7.PRN and PAY7.HEX.

(a) Write a command to assemble the MAIL.ASM file.

A> ______________

(b) What readable file is produced as output? ________________

(c) What other file is produced as output? ________________

- - - - - - - - - - - - - - - -

(a) A>ASM MAIL; (b) MAIL.PRN; (c) MAIL.HEX

8. The LOAD program is used to convert a HEX file to a COM file. This turns the file into a command file that is executable as a transient program by typing the filename and hitting RETURN. If you enter the command:

A>LOAD PAY7

the file PAY7.HEX, created by ASM PAY7, is "loaded" and translated into machine executable code. The output is then filed on disk as PAY7.COM. You can now enter PAY7 and run the program.

As you can see, if you know how to write programs in 8080 Assembler Language, this method will enable you to create new transient programs that run under CP/M.

(a) What filetype is needed for input to LOAD? ________________

(b) Write a command to load the file produced by ASM MAIL.

A> ________________

(c) What file will contain the output? ________________

- - - - - - - - - - - - - - - - -

(a) HEX; (b) A>LOAD MAIL; (c) MAIL.COM

9. Most assembler programs (in fact, most programs) don't work perfectly the first time. They need to be tested and debugged. (Debug is a quasi-technical term for "getting the bugs out," or making a program work correctly.) CP/M provides the DDT transient program as a dynamic debugging tool to help programmers debug their assembler language programs. Either HEX or COM files can be debugged with DDT. We're not going to go into details of DDT here, but assembler programmers can interact with the computer as they test and run their programs.

DDT has a side effect that is often useful for non-programmers. You can use DDT to bring *any* COM or HEX file into the TPA. Then you can use the built-in SAVE command to place it on disk – by any name and under the current user number.

(a) What are two uses of the DDT transient program? ________________

____

(b) What filetypes can be specified with the DDT command? ________________

____

- - - - - - - - - - - - - - -

(a) debug assembler programs and put a HEX or COM file in TPA; (b) COM and HEX

10. Another CP/M transient program often used with programming or debugging is DUMP. You specify DUMP like this:

DUMP specific-file-name

You can specify a file of any filetype, including HEX and COM. DUMP displays the file contents in coded form, using hexadecimal numbers. In order to read the result, you must be able to translate the hexadecimal numbers yourself. We're not going to teach you how to do that here; it's quite complex. If you're not a programmer you won't need to use DUMP displays. If you are a programmer you should already know how to interpret hexadecimal code.

If you're going to use DUMP, don't forget your CP/M control characters. ^P will turn echo printing on and off. ^S will interrupt the display. ^C will abort the DUMP display.

(a) TYPE will not show you what's in an unprintable COM file. What CP/M transient program will allow you to display the contents of an unprintable file in a "semi-readable" form? ____________

(b) DUMP displays file contents using ____________ numbers.

(c) Write the command to display the contents of the file named MAIL.COM.

____

(d) What control character will temporarily interrupt a dump display? ____________

(e) What control character will abort a dump display? ____________

(f) What control character will echo print a dump display? ____________

- - - - - - - - - - - - - - - -

(a) DUMP; (b) hexadecimal; (c) DUMP MAIL.COM; (d) ^S; (e) ^C; (f) ^P

11. Name the CP/M program (built-in or transient) that can accomplish each function below.

(a) Copy program files to a different disk. ____________

(b) Produce a hexadecimal listing of file contents. ____________

(c) Write a file consisting of a specific number of pages from the TPA. ____________

(d) Change the name of a file. ____________

(e) Convert a HEX file to a COM file. ____________

(f) Debug a HEX or COM file. ____________

(g) Bring any COM file into the TPA. ____________

____

(h) Create an ASCII (printable) file. ____________

(i) Convert an ASM file to a HEX file. ____________

(j) Determine the amount of space left on a disk. ____________

(a) PIP; (b) DUMP; (c) SAVE; (d) REN; (e) DDT and LOAD; (f) DDT; (g) DDT; (h) ED; (i) ASM; (j) STAT

SYSTEM-RELATED TRANSIENTS

Two CP/M transient programs are used for handling the system tracks on a CP/M disk; SYSGEN and MOVCPM. As you know, each CP/M disk that you use when booting (cold starting) must contain a CP/M system tailored for your equipment. SYSGEN is used to copy a working system to a new disk so you can boot with that disk as well. MOVCPM is used to change the size of CP/M. We'll see how both are used in this section.

12. The SYSGEN transient program is used to generate a new system disk. In effect, SYSGEN allows you to copy the system tracks from one disk to another. The SYSGEN program will tell you what to do after you enter the command. First SYSGEN gives you the CP/M version number and another instruction, similar to this:

```
A>SYSGEN
SYSGEN VERSION 2.0
SOURCE DRIVE NAME (OR RETURN TO SKIP)_
```

You have two choices at this point. You can enter the name of the drive from which you wish to copy the system tracks – the source of your system – or you can just hit carriage return. You need to enter a drive name, unless you have already placed a copy of CP/M in memory. You'll learn to do that with MOVCPM a bit later. For now, let's assume you want to use the system from the disk on drive A.

(a) Write the drive name as you would enter it.

```
SOURCE DRIVE NAME (OR RETURN TO SKIP)____
```

(b) What is the name of the transient program used to place CP/M system tracks on a new disk? ____________

(a) A; (b) SYSGEN

13. As soon as you enter a drive name for SYSGEN, the CCP reads and processes it, and the next line is shown. You don't need to include a colon or hit enter. Now the console shows this:

```
A>SYSGEN
SYSGEN VERSION 2.0
SOURCE DRIVE NAME (OR RETURN TO SKIP)A
SOURCE ON A, THEN TYPE RETURN_
```

The system waits to give you time to insert the desired source disk (the one you want to copy the system tracks *from*) into the A drive. If it is already on the A drive you simply hit RETURN. Otherwise you change disks on drive A – without using either a cold or warm start – then hit RETURN. The system tracks are read into memory (the TPA) and you get these messages at the console:

```
FUNCTION COMPLETE
DESTINATION DRIVE NAME (OR RETURN TO REBOOT)_
```

The system now expects you to tell which drive contains the disk into which you want to copy the system tracks. Remember that we want to place the system on the disk on our second drive. What do you enter? ________________________________

– – – – – – – – – – – – – – – –

B (no colon or carriage return)

14. After the destination drive is entered, you get this message:

```
DESTINATION ON B, THEN TYPE RETURN_
```

You can now place the destination disk on drive B, if it isn't there already, then hit RETURN. When you do, you get these messages.

```
FUNCTION COMPLETE
DESTINATION DRIVE NAME (OR RETURN TO REBOOT)_
```

This is the same set of messages you saw earlier. But now FUNCTION COMPLETE means that the destination disk contains the CP/M system from memory. You can specify another drive name if you have several disks you need to initialize with your system tracks. You can even specify the same drive again and change disks on drive B. The same system you loaded into the TPA in memory can be used as often as needed. CP/M simply copies it to each destination drive you select. When you have finished, hit RETURN. The system does a warm start and gives you the command prompt, ready for another command.

Here is a copy of a complete SYSGEN interaction:

```
1  A>SYSGEN
2  SYSGEN VER 2.2
3  SOURCE DRIVE NAME (OR RETURN TO SKIP)A
4  SOURCE ON A, THEN TYPE RETURN
5  FUNCTION COMPLETE
6  DESTINATION DRIVE NAME (OR RETURN TO REBOOT)C
7  DESTINATION ON C, THEN TYPE RETURN
8  FUNCTION COMPLETE
9  DESTINATION DRIVE NAME (OR RETURN TO REBOOT)
10 A>_
```

Use the line numbers as you answer the questions below.

(a) On which line is the source drive entered? ______________________

(b) On which line is the destination drive entered? ______________________

(c) On which lines does the system wait for you to change drives? ____________

(d) Which line indicates that the system tracks are copied to the disk on drive C?

____

(e) At which lines did the operator hit RETURN? ______________________

- - - - - - - - - - - - - - - -

(a) 3; (b) 6; (c) 4, 7; (d) 8; (e) 1, 4, 7, 9

15. You can use SYSGEN to initialize a new disk even if your system supports a single drive. Examine the sequence below.

```
A>SYSGEN
SYSGEN VER 2.2
SOURCE DRIVE NAME (OR RETURN TO SKIP)A
SOURCE ON A, THEN TYPE RETURN
FUNCTION COMPLETE
DESTINATION DRIVE NAME (OR RETURN TO REBOOT)A
DESTINATION ON A, THEN TYPE RETURN
FUNCTION COMPLETE
DESTINATION DRIVE NAME (OR RETURN TO REBOOT)
A>_
```

(a) At what point would you remove the source disk from drive A and insert the destination disk? ______________________

____

(b) What would be the result if you didn't change disks? ______________________

____

- - - - - - - - - - - - - - - -

(a) at DESTINATION ON A, before hitting RETURN; (b) no change to the disk

16. The SYSGEN program writes the system in the TPA to the system tracks of the destination disk. It doesn't touch the rest of the destination disk. If the disk was empty before SYSGEN, the directory will still be empty afterward. If you want transient programs or other files on your newly initialized disk, you use PIP to copy them.

You can also use SYSGEN to put your system tracks on a disk that contains data files. For example, you might purchase a CP/M-compatible disk containing game programs. You can copy your system tracks onto it using SYSGEN. This will not interfere with the directory or data on the disk. It will enable you to boot with that disk if necessary. As you may recall, you can boot (cold start) your machine only with a disk containing CP/M system tracks for your system on drive A.

(a) How does a SYSGEN operation affect the directory of the destination disk?

____

(b) Under what circumstances can you use a disk without your CP/M system tracks?

____

(c) Does initializing an empty disk differ from copying your system to a disk containing data? ________________ If so, how? ________________

____

- - - - - - - - - - - - - - - -

(a) it doesn't touch the directory; (b) if you don't boot with it; (c) no difference

17. When you use SYSGEN, you might make certain errors. If you enter a drive name that your system doesn't recognize, such as a number, you'll get a message like this one for version 1.4:

INVALID DRIVE NAME (USE A, B, C OR D)

followed by a repeat of the request for source or destination drive. Of course, version 2.0 supports more drive names. The INVALID message will be repeated every time you enter a drive name your system doesn't recognize.

Suppose you are working with a system that has two drives and you accidentally enter D as the destination drive. You get the second message below:

```
    DESTINATION DRIVE NAME (OR RETURN TO REBOOT)D
===> DESTINATION ON D, THEN TYPE RETURN_
```

The system has recognized the drive name, but it hasn't yet noticed that it doesn't actually have a D drive. Since you don't have a D drive, you can't put your destination disk on it. If you hit RETURN, you get a disk error message or your system hangs up, depending on your hardware. You may need to boot (cold start) and begin the SYSGEN program again. You get a similar response when you try to use either source or destination drive without a disk loaded. If you notice an error before CP/M does, you can use ^C to terminate SYSGEN at any point.

Suppose you are using a version 2.2 system that may support up to 16 drives (A through P). Only six are actually attached, however. What sort of error message would you get from each sequence below?

(a) SOURCE DRIVE NAME (OR RETURN TO SKIP)V

____

(b) SOURCE DRIVE NAME (OR RETURN TO SKIP)J
SOURCE ON J, THEN TYPE RETURN

____

(c) How could you have avoided the error message in (b) after you have entered drive J? _______________

- - - - - - - - - - - - - - - -

(a) INVALID DRIVE NAME; (b) a disk error or system hangup; (c) enter ^C instead of carriage return

18. You have seen how to use SYSGEN to copy your system tracks from one disk to another. Let's review the process. Suppose you have four disk drives. You want to put the system from the disk currently in the A drive on two new disks. You will use drive B for both new disks, since that one is easier to reach from your console. At the start you have your master CP/M system disk on drive A and an empty disk on drive B. Make the appropriate entries and answer the questions below.

(a) A> _______________

(b) SYSGEN VER 2.2
SOURCE DRIVE NAME (OR RETURN TO SKIP) _______________

(c) SOURCE ON A, THEN TYPE RETURN

What must you do before you type RETURN?

____

(d) FUNCTION COMPLETE

What function is complete at this point?

____

(e) DESTINATION DRIVE NAME (OR RETURN TO REBOOT) _______________

(f) DESTINATION ON B, THEN TYPE RETURN

What must you do before you type RETURN?

____

(g) FUNCTION COMPLETE

What function is complete at this point?

____

(h) DESTINATION DRIVE NAME (OR RETURN TO REBOOT) __________

(i) DESTINATION ON B, THEN TYPE RETURN

What must you do before you type RETURN?

____

(j) FUNCTION COMPLETE
DESTINATION DRIVE NAME (OR RETURN TO REBOOT)

How do you terminate SYSGEN? ______________________________

- - - - - - - - - - - - - - - - -

(a) SYSGEN; (b) A; (c) nothing; (d) the system is in the TPA; (e) B; (f) nothing; (g) the system is on the disk in drive B; (h) B; (i) change disk; (j) hit RETURN

19. Usually we put the CP/M system on every disk we use. That way we can boot with any disk. It doesn't take up any usable data area, so it may as well be there.

CP/M is copyrighted by Digital Research. When you purchase the master disk from Digital Research or an authorized dealer and sign the registration card, you have the right to make up to five copies *for one computer system.* If you make copies to use on another microcomputer, you're violating Digital Research's copyright.

You should label every disk that contains the CP/M system tracks with the same copyright notice on your CP/M master diskette. This label can be your signal that the disk contains the system tracks.

When you purchase a fresh disk, what two steps should you take to initialize it?

(a) ______________________________

(b) ______________________________

- - - - - - - - - - - - - - - - -

(a) put the system tracks on using SYSGEN; (b) add the copyright label

Later on you'll learn some other steps we take to initialize a new disk.

20. The MOVCPM transient program is used to move a CP/M system into memory and to alter its size. In the process, you can tailor the system to whatever size you need to work with. From there you can execute the system (warm start), create a COM file, or initialize a disk using SYSGEN. After your initial command, the CCP gives you messages about what it is doing. MOVCPM allows two operands and its effect depends on the operands you use. The first operand can be omitted or it can state the size of the system you want.

MOVCPM	Constructs and executes a CP/M system the maximum size for your hardware.
MOVCPM 32	Constructs and executes a 32K system.

If you specify a memory size larger than the one in your computer, the results are unpredictable. If the system "hangs up" you might have to boot before you can continue using CP/M. If your actual memory size is 32K or larger, the example above will result in screen messages like these:

```
A>MOVCPM 32
CONSTRUCTING 32K DOS VERS 2.0
ENTERY FOR HARD DISK SYSTEM
32K DOS VERS 2.0

A>_
```

If your microcomputer includes a hard disk, you'll enter Y after the question. Otherwise you'll use a carriage return as we have here. Suppose you have a CP/M disk configured for 32K on your A drive. Your machine has 48K memory.

(a) What command will construct a 48K system and execute it?

____

(b) What command will configure the system you have and perform an automatic warm start? __________________________________

(c) What would happen if you enter MOVCPM 84?

____

- - - - - - - - - - - - - - - -

(a) MOVCPM or MOVCPM 48; (b) MOVCPM 32; (c) a synchronization error; you must cold start

21. There could be a number of reasons why you would want to change your memory size. Perhaps you've expanded your computer with another 16K memory board. You don't have to buy a new CP/M; just tell your existing system about your new memory size.

Another reason might be that you've bought a transient program that requires a reserved memory area at the top of memory. We have one program that requires 1K of memory to be set aside outside of CP/M. Therefore all of our system disks say 63K instead of 64K, which is what we really have. Thus, our memory architecture is:

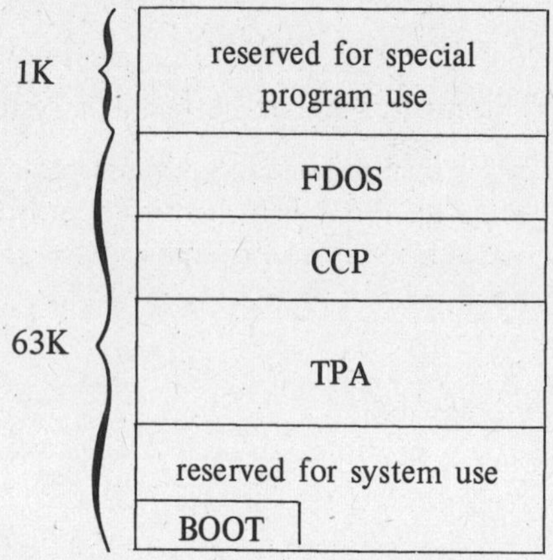

If you buy such a program, its documentation should tell you exactly what to do.

Suppose you have just expanded your system from 32K to 48K. You have five disks already containing your old 32K system.

(a) Do you need to buy a new CP/M system disk? ______________

(b) What CP/M program can be used to reconfigure your memory size? ______

(c) What CP/M program can be used to copy your new system to all your five disks?

____

- - - - - - - - - - - - - - - - -

(a) no; (b) MOVCPM; (c) SYSGEN

22. The command MOVCPM, with no operands, constructs a maximum size system for your computer and executes it immediately. Why would you do this? Suppose you have a 64K memory but all your disks are configured to 63K, like ours. You can temporarily use all 64K by using the MOVCPM command. You can also switch back to 63K by a cold start or by entering MOVCPM 63.

If the system that's stored on your disks is less than your maximum memory size, there's usually some reason. Exercise caution in making a change.

Suppose your system has 32K bytes of main memory. You have booted from a disk that contains a system configured for 20K bytes. The disk also contains the file MOVCPM.COM.

(a) Write a command to temporarily switch to a 32K system.

A> ______________________________

(b) Write a command to temporarily switch to a 25K system.

A> ______________________________

(c) Show two ways to return to the 20K system.

____

____

(d) Suppose you don't know what size memory your computer has. How can you find out? ____

____

____

- - - - - - - - - - - - - - -

(a) MOVCPM or MOVCPM 32; (b) MOVCPM 25; (c) MOVCPM 20 or a cold start; (d) enter MOVCPM with no operands and you'll get a message like this:

```
CONSTRUCTING DOS nnK SYSTEM
CP/M DOS nnK VERS n.n
```

"*nnK*" tells you the size of main memory

23. As you have seen, the first operand of MOVCPM is used to change the memory size or use your system's maximum. The second operand is used to specify where you want the new system to go.

If you omit the second operand, the new system is automatically rebooted and takes effect immediately. You might want to do this if you are only making a temporary memory size change for the purpose of one job.

If you include the second operand, which is merely an asterisk (*), the new system remains in the TPA and is not executed. You would do this if you want to write the new system onto one or more disks.

MOVCPM 32 would move a copy of the system tracks from the active disk into the TPA, change the memory size to 32K, and reboot using the new system size.

MOVCPM 32 * would move a copy of the system tracks from the active disk into the TPA, change the memory size to 32K, and wait for further instructions.

(a) Write a command to load the system into the TPA, change the memory size to 40K, and keep the new system in the TPA.

A> ____

(b) Write a command to load the system into the TPA, change the memory size to 63K, and reboot immediately using the new system.

A> ____

(c) Suppose you're using a transient program that requires a memory size of 2K less than your full memory size. Suppose that your full memory size is 48K. You don't want to make a permanent change to any of your disks but want to change the size right now so you can use this program. What CP/M command would you enter?

A> ____

(d) When you're done with the above job, how can you get back to the 48K memory size again? (There are several possible correct answers to this question.)

____

____

____

(e) Suppose you've added 16K to your computer so that you now have 64K. You want to change the system tracks of all your disks to the new size. What MOVCPM command would you enter?

A> ____

(f) Would any of the above commands affect the system tracks of the active disk?

______________ If so, which ones? ______________________________

- - - - - - - - - - - - - - - -

(a) A>MOVCPM 40 *; (b) A>MOVCPM 63; (c) A>MOVCPM 46; (d) you could enter A>MOVCPM 48 or just A>MOVCPM or you could boot the system from disk again; (e) A>MOVCPM 64 * will keep the new system in the TPA so that you can SYSGEN it onto your disks; (f) no – only SYSGEN does that

24. When the new system is left in the TPA, you get a message like this:

```
READY FOR "SYSGEN" OR "SAVE nn CPMxx.COM"
A>_
```

We'll discuss each of these alternatives in turn.

If you want to copy the new system onto some disks, use the SYSGEN command.

```
A>SYSGEN
SYSGEN VER 2.2
SOURCE DRIVE NAME (OR RETURN TO SKIP)_
```

Do you remember what happens now? If you enter a valid drivename, the system is loaded into the TPA from the selected disk. However, if you hit return without entering a drivename, it's assumed that *the system is already in the TPA.*

Since you've just used MOVCPM to create a new system in the TPA, you should definitely use the system that's in the TPA already. You just hit return, then you can specify as many destination disks as you want.

Suppose you want to change the disk on A drive from a 64K system to a 63K system. Show the commands you would enter.

(a) A> ______________________________

```
CONSTRUCTING 63K DOS VERS 2.2
READY FOR "SYSGEN" OR "SAVE 34 CPM63.COM"
```

(b) A>______________________________

```
SYSGEN VERS 2.2
```

(c) `SOURCE DRIVE NAME (OR RETURN TO SKIP)`__________

(d) `DESTINATION DRIVE NAME (OR RETURN TO REBOOT)`__________
`FUNCTION COMPLETE`

(e) `DESTINATION DRIVE NAME (OR RETURN TO REBOOT)`__________

`A>`__________

- - - - - - - - - - - - - - - -

(a) A>MOVCPM 63* (the asterisk is important as it causes MOVCPM to save the new system and wait for a SYSGEN or SAVE command); (b) A>SYSGEN; (c) return only; (d) A; (e) return only

25. The response to MOVCPM xx * is

```
READY FOR "SYSGEN" OR "SAVE nn CPMxx.COM"
```

You've seen how the SYSGEN command is used. The SAVE command is used to create a COM file containing the system from the TPA. "nn" tells you the exact number of pages to save. This will vary for different computers and even for different size versions. You'll see the exact number of pages you need to save.

Why would you want a COM file containing the CP/M system? Ordinarily you wouldn't, but if you want to DUMP the system, or if you want to change it using DDT, then you need the COM file. You'll only want to do this if you're tailoring your system and you know 8080 Assembler Language.

Show the commands to create a 32K system and save it as a COM file.

(a) A> __________

```
CONSTRUCTING 32K DOS VERS 2.2
READY FOR "SYSGEN" OR "SAVE 32 CPM32.COM"
```

(b) A> __________

- - - - - - - - - - - - - - - -

(a) A>MOVCPM 32 *; (b) SAVE 32 CPM32.COM

26. When you're trying to make a COM file, you may want to use the maximum system size your equipment supports. The first operand can be an asterisk.

A>MOVCPM * *

The above command means to construct a system of the maximum size from the active drive and wait for further instructions. Note that MOVCPM * (just one asterisk) wouldn't work because the system interprets the scle asterisk as the first operand. It would construct a maximum size system and automatically reboot.

Write a set of commands to save the 20K system from drive A as a COM file.

(a) A> __________

____

```
READY FOR "SYSGEN" OR "SAVE 30 CPM20.COM"
```

(b) A> ____________________

Suppose the A drive contains a 32K system disk and the B drive contains a 30K system disk. Both disks contain the MOVCPM.COM file. You have booted from A and are currently using the 32K system. Show the command to load the 30K system and reboot from it – without changing disks.

(c) A> ____________________

- - - - - - - - - - - - - - - -

(a) A>MOVCPM 20 *; (b) A>SAVE 30 CPM20.COM; (c) A>MOVCPM 30

27. You've seen a lot of different options of MOVCPM and SYSGEN. Let's review the various things you can do.

The full format of the MOVCPM command is:

```
d>MOVCPM [nn] [*]
         [* ]
```

With no operands, the maximum size system is constructed in the TPA and immediately executed.

The first operand gives a new system size, which must be less than or equal to the actual memory size. An asterisk means to construct a maximum size CP/M. It's only used when the second operand is also used.

The second operand tells what to do with the system in the TPA. If omitted, the system automatically boots from the version in the TPA. If the second operand is included the system does not boot, but puts out the following message and waits for further instructions.

```
READY FOR "SYSGEN" OR "SAVE nn CPMxx.COM"
```

The SAVE command will make a COM file out of the system. You usually only do this if you're tailoring your system.

SYSGEN copies the system onto the system tracks of a designated destination disk. The source can be either the TPA or another disk. To use the TPA as the source, don't type a source drive. To use a disk as the source, type the appropriate drivename.

Suppose you want to temporarily use a 30K memory size.

(a) What command would you enter? A> ____________________

(b) How can you go back to your maximum size? ____________________

____

Suppose your disk in drive A has a 64K system (the maximum for your hardware) and you want to change it to a 60K system. Show the commands you would use.

(c) A>____________________

____

```
CONSTRUCTING 60K DOS VERS 2.2
READY FOR "SYSGEN" OR "SAVE 34 CPM60.COM"
```

(d) A>______________________________

```
SYSGEN VER 2.2
```

(e) SOURCE DRIVE NAME (OR RETURN TO SKIP)________________

(f) DESTINATION DRIVE NAME (OR RETURN TO REBOOT)________________
FUNCTION COMPLETE

(g) DESTINATION DRIVE NAME (OR RETURN TO REBOOT)________________

Suppose you want to construct a 30K system and save it as a COM file on the A disk. Show the commands you would use.

(h) A> ______________________________

```
CONSTRUCTING 30K DOS VERS 2.2
READY FOR "SYSGEN" OR "SAVE 32 CPM30.COM"
```

(i) A> ______________________________

(j) Change your command in (h) above so the system size is at a maximum.

A> ______________________________

Suppose you want to copy the system from the B disk onto the A disk. Show the commands you would use.

(k) A>______________________________

(l) SYSGEN VER 2.2
SOURCE DRIVE NAME (OR RETURN TO SKIP)________________
FUNCTION COMPLETE

(m) DESTINATION DRIVE NAME (OR RETURN TO REBOOT)________________
FUNCTION COMPLETE

(n) DESTINATION DRIVE NAME (OR RETURN TO REBOOT)________________

\- - - - - - - - - - - - - - - -

(a) A>MOVCPM 30; (b) MOVCPM with no operands; (c) A>MOVCPM 60 *; (d) SYSGEN; (e) return; (f) A; (g) return; (h) A>MOVCPM 30 *; (i) SAVE 32 CPM30.COM; (j) A>MOVCPM * *; (k) SYSGEN; (l) B; (m) A; (n) return

CP/M TRANSIENTS

28. Any CP/M transient program reference can be prefixed by a drivename. This causes the program to be loaded from the named drive instead of the current drive. Thus, A>B:SYSGEN will invoke the SYSGEN program from the disk on the B drive. A remains the active drive, and CP/M will return to drive A after SYSGEN is finished. A>B:ASM ABC will load the ASM program from drive B and assemble program

ABC.ASM from drive A. The drivename can precede any transient program name. If the program COM file does not exist on the specified (or default) drive, CP/M will question the command and return a drive prompt such as A>.

For each command below, indicate from which drive the CP/M transient program will be loaded.

(a) A>MOVCPM ____________________

(b) A>B:MOVCPM ____________________

(c) B>MOVCPM ____________________

(d) B>A:MOVCPM ____________________

Suppose you have this CP/M interaction:

```
A>MOVCPM 32 *
MOVCPM?

A>_
```

(e) What's wrong? ____________________

- - - - - - - - - - - - - - - -

(a) A; (b) B; (c) B; (d) A; (e) the A disk does not contain the file MOVCPM.COM

In this chapter we have looked briefly at the transient programs provided by Digital Research as part of the CP/M system disk. We looked at the system-related transients, and you learned to generate a new CP/M system of the appropriate size using MOVCPM and/or SYSGEN. Now you know all there is to know about these two programs.

We looked briefly at the programming-related transients. You saw what type of files can be operated on by ASM, LOAD, and DDT. You saw how to produce a hexadecimal dump of any file using the DUMP transient. We won't deal with programming anymore in this book.

We overviewed programs used for status information, file management, creating or changing files, and running a series of CP/M commands. The rest of this book deals with the STAT, PIP, ED, and SUBMIT programs in detail. You'll learn to use all their options as you continue.

Your master CP/M disk may contain other transient program files. Some of these are supplies by Digital Research for use in tailoring the system. Others may have been added by your CP/M suppliers. Your documentation should explain exactly what these files are and how they are used. Look also for any files of type DOC, PRN, or MSG. TYPE such files and you may find additional documentation.

CHAPTER 4 SELF-TEST

This Self-Test will help you determine if you have mastered the objectives of this chapter. Answer each question to the best of your ability, then check your answers in the answer key at the end of the test.

1. Name the CP/M program that accomplishes each function described below.

   (a) Determine how much space is left on a disk.

   ____

   (b) Copy a file to another disk.

   ____

   (c) Create a new file.

   ____

   (d) Run a series of CP/M programs with one command.

   ____

   (e) Change the name of a file.

   ____

2. Which of the CP/M programs in question 1 would be located in the system tracks of a CP/M disk? ______________________________

drive A	drive B
PIP.COM	SALES.ASM
ED.COM	SALES.DAT
SYSGEN.COM	ASM.COM
DUMP.COM	LOAD.COM
MOVCPM.COM	DDT.COM

Figure 4.1

Figure 4.1 shows the transient programs contained on two disks. The following questions refer to these.

3. Write a command to create a HEX file and a PRN file from the assembler source code in SALES.ASM.

   B> ______________________________

4. Write a command to create a COM file from the HEX file.

   B> ______________________________

5. How can you obtain a printed listing of the PRN file?

____

6. Produce a hexadecimal listing of the SALES.ASM file at the console.

B> ______________________________

7. Suppose you want to copy the system tracks from the disk on drive A to a new disk on drive C.

(a) What drive will you use? ______________

(b) What command do you enter first? ______________

(c) What source drivename will you enter? ______________

(d) What destination drivename will you enter? ______________

8. Suppose you want to configure a 48K system and place a copy of it on drive C as a COM file. You also want to place the 48K system on the disk in drive D.

(a) Write the first command you need? A> ______________

(b) The response you get is this;

```
READY FOR "SYSGEN" OR "SAVE 32 CPM48.COM"
```

How do you create a COM file on drive C?

A> ______________________________

(c) How do you write the system tracks to the disk on drive D?

____

9. Write a command to configure and execute a temporary 32K CP/M system.

____

Chapter 4 Answer Key

Compare your answers to the Self-Test with the correct answers given below. If all your answers are correct you are ready to go on to the next chapter. If you missed any questions, you may find it helpful to review the appropriate frames in this chapter.

1. (a) STAT
   (b) PIP
   (c) ED
   (d) SUBMIT
   (e) REN

2. REN only. The rest are transient programs.

3. ASM SALES

4. LOAD SALES

5. TYPE SALES.PRN with ^P or use PIP to copy SALES.PRN to the printer.

6. A:DUMP SALES.ASM (or you could TYPE SALES.HEX) These produce different formats, but both will be in HEX.

7. (a) A
   (b) SYSGEN
   (c) A
   (d) C

8. (a) MOVCPM 48 *
   (b) SAVE 32 C:CPM48.COM
   (c) use SYSGEN, but don't enter a source drive

9. MOVCPM 32

Machine Exercise Suggestions

In this machine exercise you'll practice with SYSGEN and MOVCPM. Use a copy of your master CP/M disk in drive A. If you have a fresh disk, use it as the destination disk. Otherwise, use any other disk that contains the same system tracks as your master disk.

1. Start up the system and boot. Notice in the boot message what size CP/M you have.

2. Check the directory of your A disk. You'll need these program files during this exercise:

   DUMP.COM
   SYSGEN.COM
   MOVCPM.COM

   If your disk doesn't contain all these files, find one that does and boot again.

3. Copy the system from the master disk to a destination disk.

4. Make a COM file of the system on disk A. Store the COM file on A.
   a. Use MOVCPM to move the system into the TPA.
   b. Use SAVE to save it as a COM file.
   c. Check your directory on A. Is CPMxx.COM there?

5. DUMP the COM file. Practice using ^S to interrupt and restart the dump. You don't need to wait for the entire dump. When you've seen what the dump looks like, abort the program.

6. Erase the COM file you created in 4 above.

7. On your *other* disk, create a 20K system.
   a. Use MOVCPM to create the 20K system.
   b. Use SYSGEN to store it.

8. Put the 20K system disk in A and boot. Your boot message should now say 20K.

9. Replace the 20K system tracks with the correct system tracks (from your master disk).

10. Boot from both disks. They should both show the same system size. That's enough for now. Shut down your system and go on to Chapter 5.

CHAPTER FIVE

The STAT Command

This chapter covers the STAT program which you can use to display or change the status of various files and devices. For example, STAT can be used to change the status of a disk from read/write to read/only.

The STAT program has several functions. For peripheral devices it can display or change device assignments, or display a table of permitted assignments. For disks, STAT can display remaining space, display read/write status, and for 2.0 and later versions, display active user numbers.

STAT can also be used to display the size of files on the disk. In later versions of CP/M, STAT can display or change the read/write status as well as display or change the system status of files. You'll learn what these mean in this chapter. STAT can display the characteristics of the disk drives and even display a STAT command summary in the later versions of CP/M.

When you have finished studying this chapter, you will be able to:

- Write STAT commands to display the status of the various devices.
- Interpret status displays produced by the various STAT functions.
- Write STAT commands to change the read/write status of a disk.
- Write STAT commands to change device assignments.

And if you're working with a newer system:

- Write STAT commands to change whether files appear in the directory.
- Write STAT commands to alter files from read/write or read/only status.
- Write STAT commands to identify user information on a disk.

First we'll look at STAT features for earlier versions of CP/M. Then we'll discuss the additional features added at version 2.0. We'll start with device assignments.

DEVICE ASSIGNMENTS

1. When a program wants to write data on the printer, it will say "write on LST:," not "write on printer." BDOS has a table that says "LST:=printer." LST: is a logical device and the printer is a physical device. CON: is a logical device and the corresponding physical device is the CRT:. If you use a teletype console, it may be assigned to both LST: and CON:.

Suppose you change your console type from a teletype to a CRT, or add a paper tape reader and punch. CP/M can be tailored so you can change your logical device assignments. You won't need to get a new version of CP/M and no one will have to rewrite your other programs.

(a) Which of the following describes a logical device?

______ An actual piece of hardware such as the line printer or CRT.

______ A functional name such as console or list device.

______ Any device containing its own memory area.

______ The CPU.

(b) BDOS maintains a table that sets logical devices equal to ____________.

(c) Logical device assignments are (fixed/changeable) ____________.

- - - - - - - - - - - - - - - -

(a) a functional name such as console or list device; (b) physical devices;
(c) changeable

2. CP/M recognizes four logical devices.

CON: This is the operator's console. The CCP sends messages to this device and reads commands from it.
RDR: This is an input device that some programs may use to read data.
PUN: This is an output device that some programs may use to write data. PUN stands for "punch."
LST: This is the output listing device. Most programs send print data to this device.

(a) When you sit down at your terminal to communicate with CP/M, which logical device are you using? ____________

(b) When you use ^P to turn on echo printing, which logical device does the echo printing? ____________

(c) If your system had a paper tape reader, which logical device would it be?

____

- - - - - - - - - - - - - - - -

(a) CON: (b) LST: (c) RDR:

CP/M can be modified to allow you to change device assignments at the console using the STAT transient program. Since this modification isn't made in all systems, we've discussed it briefly in Appendix A.

DISK STATUS

3. The command STAT, with no operands, displays the read/write status and amount of space available on each disk. A typical interaction is:

```
A>STAT
A:R/W, SPACE: 157K
B:R/O, SPACE: 118K
A>_
```

What does the read/write status tell you? Under CP/M you can protect an important disk from being accidentally erased or written over by giving it a read/only status. You can read from the disk, but you can't write on it.

When you first install a disk on a non-A drive, it automatically receives a read/only status. ^C, the warm start, changes the status to read/write. If you want to use the read/only status, enter STAT d:=R/O, where *d* is the drive name.

(a) What command produced this output? ______________________

```
A:R/O, SPACE: 121K
B:R/W, SPACE: 118K
```

(b) Can you write on the disk in A drive? ______________________

(c) Can you read from the disk in A drive? ______________________

(d) Can you erase files from the disk in A drive? ______________________

(e) Can you write on the disk in B drive? ______________________

(f) Can you read from the disk in B drive? ______________________

(g) Can you erase files from the disk in B drive? ______________________

(h) How much room is available on disk A? ______________________

(i) How much room is available on disk B? ______________________

(j) Suppose you change the disk in B drive. What read/write status does the new disk have? __________ How can you change the status? __________

(k) Write the command to change the disk on B from R/W to R/O status.

____

- - - - - - - - - - - - - - -

____

(a) STAT (with no operands); (b) no; (c) yes; (d) no; (e) yes; (f) yes; (g) yes; (h) 121K bytes; (i) 118K bytes; (j) R/O, ^C; (k) STAT B:=R/O

4. If you try to write on an R/O disk, you'll get this message;

```
BDOS ERR ON d: R/O_
```

The system will wait for *any* response. The instant you type something, the system will reboot, automatically giving all disks R/W status. You'll then lose the R/O status and must re-establish it, if you want it.

(a) What does this message mean: BDOS ERR ON A: R/O_

____

____

(b) How do you continue after this message?

____

____

(c) What effect will your action have on the read/write status of the disks?

____

- - - - - - - - - - - - - - -

(a) you tried to write on a disk that was read/only; (b) type any character; (c) all disks become R/W

5. The command STAT displays both the read/write status and the amount of available space on all disks. If you just want to find out the amount of available space on a specific drive, use this command format:

STAT d:

The output will look like this:

```
BYTES REMAINING ON d: nnnK
```

(a) What command produced this message shown below? ____________________

```
BYTES REMAINING ON B: 124K
```

(b) Suppose you want to put a new file on disk A, and you're not sure there's enough room. How can you find out? ____________________

- - - - - - - - - - - - - - -

(a) STAT B; (b) STAT A: or STAT

6. (a) Write a command to display the space on disk B.

____

(b) Write a command to display the read/write status of all drives as well as the amount of available space. _______________

(c) Write a command to change drive B to R/O status.

____

(d) What do you type to change all disks to R/W status?

____

- - - - - - - - - - - - - - -

(a) STAT B:; (b) STAT; (c) STAT B:=R/O; (d) ^C (system reboot)

The preceding frames have covered the STAT functions for disk status. STAT also provides several functions for individual files on a disk.

FILE STATUS

7. STAT will display the size of a file. The command format is: STAT filename. Here's an example:

```
A>STAT PIP.COM

RECS BYTS EX D:FILENAME.TYP
  55   7K  1 A:PIP.COM
```

The output shows that PIP.COM contains 55 records, takes up 7K bytes, and uses one disk extent. (A disk extent is a 16K-byte block.)

(a) What command produced the message shown below?

```
RECS BYTS EX D:FILENAME.TYP
 178  23K  2 B:INVENTY.DAT
```

____

(b) What does "EX" stand for? _______________

(c) If a file had 60K bytes, how many disk extents would you expect it to use?

____

- - - - - - - - - - - - - - -

(a) STAT B:INVENTY.DAT; (b) extent; (c) 4

8. In the command STAT filename, the filename can be generalized. STAT will list the status of all files on the selected disk that match the general filename and also give the amount of available space on disk. The files will be listed in alphabetical order.

Here's an example:

```
A>STAT *.COM

RECS  BYTS  EX   D:FILENAME.TYP
  60    8K   1   A:COPY.COM
  11    2K   1   A:DAR.COM
  55    7K   1   A:PIP.COM
 178   23K   2   A:WS.COM

BYTES REMAINING ON A: 116K
```

(a) In the above example, how many records does COPY.COM contain? ________

(b) How many extents does WS.COM use? ________

(c) How much space is available on the A disk? ________

(d) Write a command to find the status of all files on B disk that start with the letters INV.

A> ________

(e) Write a command to display the status of all files on A.

A> ________

(f) Show three different commands to find out the amount of space remaining on A.

A> ________

A> ________

A> ________

(g) Which of the above commands is the most efficient if you just want to find out the available space? A> ________

- - - - - - - - - - - - - -

(a) 60: (b) 2; (c) 116K bytes; (d) A>STAT B:INV?????.* or STAT B:INV*.*; (e) A>STAT*.*; (f) A>STAT A: or A>STAT or A>STAT *.*; (g) A>STAT A:

STAT FOR VERSION 2.0

So far the STAT commands you have studied pertain to CP/M versions before release 2.0. If you are working with an earlier version, skip the remaining frames and go on to the Self-Test for this chapter. If you have version 2.0 or later, continue with frame 9.

9. Read/write protection has been enhanced with release 2.0. It is now available on a file-by-file basis and for the disk as a whole. The read/write status for each file is stored with the file directory entry.

When you create a new file it is assumed to have read/write status. To change the status enter this command:

STAT filename $R/O

The filename may be specific or general. File status is not affected by ^C, as the disk status is.

To change the status back to read/write, use this command:

STAT filename $R/W

Notice that at least one space precedes the status operand (R/O and R/W) and that it begins with a dollar sign.

STAT lists the changed file(s) on the console.

(a) When a new file is created what is its status? ______________

(b) Write a command to set the status of A:INVENTY.DAT to read/only.

A> ______________

(c) How can INVENTY.DAT be reset to read/write status?

A> ______________

(d) Write a command to set the entire disk on B drive to read/only status.

A> ______________

(e) Write a command to set all the files on B disk to read/only status.

A> ______________

- - - - - - - - - - - - - - - -

(a) R/W; (b) A>STAT INVENTY.DAT $R/O; (c) STAT INVENTY.DAT $R/W; (d) A>STAT B:=R/O; (e) A>STAT B:*.* $R/O

10. Another feature of version 2.0 allows you to declare *system* files. A system file is not listed in the directory when you enter DIR. However, it is still related to a user number. Only the files of the active user number are identified by STAT.

When you use CP/M, you'll usually need a set of files that might include PIP.COM, STAT.COM, and ED.COM. Since you know these are available to you they don't need to be in a directory listing. You can make them system files.

System status bears no relationship to read/write status. A system file can be written on or erased as long as it has R/W status.

(a) If you log on as USER 1 and then enter A>DIR, what will be listed?

a. All files on A disk linked to user 1.

b. All files on all disks related to user 1.

c. All files on A disk regardless of user number.

d. All files on A disk linked to user 1 except for system files.

(b) Can you erase a system file? ______________________

\- - - - - - - - - - - - - - - -

(a) d; (b) yes, as long as it has R/W status

11. Because a file is called a "system" file does not make it a part of the system tracks. It's still a separate file and must be separately copied to each disk that you want it on.

Suppose you want to initialize each new disk with the system tracks and these system files: PIP.COM, ED.COM, STAT.COM, and P3.TEX, which is a user 0 file.

(a) How do you copy the system tracks? ______________________

(b) How do you copy the system files? ______________________

(c) How do you copy the user file? ______________________

\- - - - - - - - - - - - - - - -

(a) SYSGEN; (b) PIP; (c) PIP

12. To give a file system status, use this command:

STAT filename $SYS

To remove system status, use this command:

STAT filename $DIR

The filename can be specific or generalized. STAT will tell you which filenames were set by the command to SYS or DIR.

(a) Write a command to make A:PIP.COM a system file.

A> ______________________

(b) Write a command to make all the COM files on disk B system files.

A> ______________________

(c) Write a command to make all files on A system files.

A> ______________________

\- - - - - - - - - - - - - - - -

(a) A>STAT PIP.COM $SYS; (b) A>STAT B:*.COM $SYS; (c) A>STAT *.* $SYS

13. You saw before that the command STAT ED.COM produces output in this format:

```
RECS  BYTS  EX  D:FILENAME.TYP
  48    6K   1  A:ED.COM
```

This has changed slightly with version 2.0. The output now may look like this:

```
RECS  BYTS  EX  ACC
  48    6K   1  R/O (A:ED.COM)
```

ACC means "access" and gives the read/write status of the file. This example is read/only (R/O). Parentheses around the filename indicate that it has system status. If the file were not a system file, parentheses would not appear.

(a) Write a command to display the size, read/write status, and system status of all COM files on A disk. A> ________________

(b) Write a command to display the read/write status of B:INVENTY.DAT.

A> ________________

(c) Suppose you have forgotten what system files are on A disk. DIR won't tell you. Write a command that will. A> ________________

(d) In the output from (c), how can you identify a system file? ________________

____

____

(e) Suppose you enter one of the above commands and get this message: STAT?

What's wrong? ________________

____

____

- - - - - - - - - - - - - - -

(a) A>STAT *.COM; (b) A>STAT B:INVENTY.DAT; (c) A>STAT *.*; (d) by parentheses around the filename; (e) the CCP can't find the STAT.COM file on A disk; it's either not there or not available to your user number.

14. The file status display may also have a SIZE field, as shown in the following interaction:

```
A>STAT *.DAT $S

SIZE  RECS  BYTS  EX  ACC  D:FILENAME.TYP
 200   200   25K   2  R/W  A:INVENTY.DAT
 100   100   12K   1  R/W  A:PARTS.DAT
```

The SIZE field gives the file size in records. It will match the RECS field unless the file is random access. Since the subject of random access files is beyond the scope of this book, the SIZE field will not be discussed further.

(a) To display the SIZE field, what operand do you use? ____________________

(b) Is the file SIZE given in bytes or records? ____________________

- - - - - - - - - - - - - - - -

(a) $S; (b) records

15. The preceding section has discussed the various STAT options for filc status. Thc general command format is:

STAT filename [$R/O $R/W $SYS $DIR $S]

With no status operands the status of the file is displayed. The $S operand also causes the SIZE to be displayed. The $R/O, $R/W, $SYS, and $DIR operands change the status of the file.

(a) Write a command to display the status of B:SORT.COM.

A> ____________________

(b) Rewrite the command in (a) to include the SIZE field in the display.

A> ____________________

(c) Write a command to display the status of all files on A disk that start with INV.

A> ____________________

(d) What will the display from (c) tell you?

_____ a. The size of the files.

_____ b. The number of bytes remaining on the disk.

_____ c. The read/write status of the files.

_____ d. The system status of the files.

_____ e. The user number of the files.

(e) Write a command to make all files on B disk system files.

A> ____________________

(f) Write a command to make all COM files on A disk read/only.

A> ____________________

(g) Write a command to display the names of all system files on B disk.

A> ____________________

(h) Examine this listing:

```
RECS  BYTS  EX  ACC   D:FILENAME.TYP
  38    5K   1  R/O   B:DDT.COM
   4    1K   1  R/W   B:DUMP.COM
  14    2K   1  R/O   (B:LOAD.COM)
  55    7K   1  R/W   B:PIP.COM
```

Which files are system files?

____

____

- - - - - - - - - - - - - - - -

(a) A>STAT B:SORT.COM; (b) A>STAT B:SORT.COM $S; (c) A>STAT INV*.*; (d) a, b, c, d; (e) A>STAT B:*.* $SYS; (f) A>STAT *.COM $R/O; (g) A>STAT B:*.*; (h) B:LOAD.COM

USER STATUS

16. The command STAT USR: causes the current user number to be displayed. It also tells you what user numbers are linked to files on the active disk. Here's an example:

```
A>STAT USR:

ACTIVE USER :  1
ACTIVE FILES:  0 1 2 5

A>_
```

The display tells you that you're logged on as user 1. The A disk contains files belonging to users 0, 1, 2, and 5.

(a) What command obtained the output shown below? ________________

```
ACTIVE USER :  1
ACTIVE FILES:  0 1 2 5
```

(b) According to the above output, what's your current user number? ________

(c) What users have files on the active disk? __________________

- - - - - - - - - - - - - - - -

(a) STAT USR:; (b) 3; (c) 0, 2, and 3

17. STAT USR: can be combined with DIR to identify the user numbers of all non-system files on a disk. The following listing shows you how.

```
A>STAT USR:

ACTIVE USER :  0
ACTIVE FILES:  0 2 5

A>DIR
A: INVENTY    DAT:PARTS     DAT:INVENTY   COM

A>USER 2

A>DIR
A: PAYROLL    DAT:TAXES     DAT:PAYROLL   COM:PAYREP    COM
A: TAXRE1     COM:UPDATE    COM:QUARTER   COM

A>USER 5

A>DIR
A: INVOICES PRN
```

STAT USR: told all the user numbers on the file – in this case 0, 2, and 5. We displayed the directory under each user number. If we had wanted to see system file names as well, we would have used STAT instead of DIR. (This assumes that STAT.COM is available for every user number.)

(a) Suppose you forget what user number you're currently using. What command should you enter? A>________________________

(b) Suppose you're looking for DUMP.COM on A disk and you don't know what user number to use. You do know it is a system file. What procedure would you use to find the user linked to DUMP.COM?

____

____

____

____

____

____

- - - - - - - - - - - - - - - -

(a) A>STAT USR:

(b) First, use STAT USR: to find out what user numbers are active. Then use STAT *.* under each relevant user number until you find the file you want.

DISK STATUS

18. The command STAT d:DSK: will display the characteristics of the disk in the specified drive. If the drive is omitted, all drives are shown.

Here's an example:

```
A>STAT A:DSK:

    A: DRIVE CHARACTERISTICS
 1944: 128 BYTE RECORD CAPACITY
  243: KILOBYTE DRIVE CAPACITY
   64: 32 BYTE DIRECTORY ENTRIES
   64: CHECKED DIRECTORY ENTRIES
  128: RECORDS/EXTENT
    8: RECORD/BLOCK
   26: SECTORS/TRACK
    2: RESERVED TRACKS
```

The drive shown above has the capacity for 1944 records (each record is 128 bytes long); 243K bytes; 64 directory entries; 128 records on each extent; 8 records per block; 26 sectors per track; and 2 reserved tracks.

"Checked directory entries" tells how many directory entries your system will check to see if a new disk has been installed on the drive. The system usually checks all the directory entries for floppy disks.

You probably won't use this command very often as the information doesn't change unless you change your disk hardware.

(a) Write a command to give you the capacity of your A drive.

A> ______________________________

(b) Write a command to give you the capacity of all your drives.

A> ______________________________

- - - - - - - - - - - - - - - -

(a) A>STAT A:DSK: (b) A>STAT DSK:

STAT OPTIONS LIST

19. You've learned a lot of STAT functions. Will you have trouble remembering which format is for which function? STAT VAL: displays a list of all the STAT command formats. It looks like this:

```
Temp R/O disk: d:=R/O
Set Indicator: d:filename.typ $R/O $R/W $SYS $DIR
Disk Status  : DSK: d:DSK:
User Status  : USR:
Iobyte Assign:
CON: = TTY: CRT: BAT: UC1:
RDR: = TTY: PTR: UR1: UR2:
PUN: = TTY: PTP: UP1: UP2:
LST: = TTY: CRT: LPT: UL1:
```

Earlier versions list only the logical to physical options, like this:

```
CON: = TTY: CRT: BAT: UC1:
RDR: = TTY: PTR: UR1: UR2:
PUN: = TTY: PTP: UP1: UP2:
LST: = TTY: CRT: LPT: UL1:
```

Suppose you want to display the status of a file but you forget what command format to use. What command should you enter?

A> ______________________________

- - - - - - - - - - - - - - - -

(a) A>STAT VAL:

You have now studied all the various functions of the STAT program.

CHAPTER 5 SELF-TEST

This Self-Test will help you determine if you have mastered the objectives of this chapter. Answer each question to the best of your ability, then check your answers in the answer key at the end of the test.

1. Briefly describe what the STAT program does.

____

____

____

____

2. Examine the following interaction.

```
A>STAT
STAT?

A>_
```

What's wrong? ______________________________

____

3. Write the appropriate command for each of the following STAT functions.

   a. Display the number of bytes available on A. (Use the most efficient method.)

   A> ______________________________

   b. Make B disk read/only. A> ______________________________

c. Display the status of all COM files on A.

A>____

d. Make B disk read/write. A> ______________________________

e. Display the read/write status of B disk.

A>____

4. How do you continue after this message?

```
BDOS ERROR ON A: READ ONLY_
```

____

____

(If you are working with an earlier system, skip the rest of this self-test.)

5. Write the appropriate command for each of the following STAT functions.

a. Make PIP.COM a system file. A>______________________________

b. Make INVENTY.PRN read/only. A> ______________________________

c. Display the read/write status of SORT.COM. A>______________________________

d. Display your current user number. A> ______________________________

e. Display the characteristics of all disk drives. A>______________________________

f. Display the names of all system files on B disk. A> ______________________________

g. Review all the STAT commands. A> ______________________________

6. Write a command to find out all the user numbers on B disk.

B> ____

7. The response to your command in question 6 is:

```
ACTIVE USER :  1
ACTIVE FILES:  0 1
```

Write a sequence of commands to display directories of all non-system files on this disk.

B> ____

B> ____

B> ____

B> ____

8. (Optional.) You have learned enough facts to write a sequence of commands to erase all the files from question 7. See if you can put them all together. (Assume that there is a STAT.COM for user 0 and another STAT.COM for user 1.)

B> ______________________________

B> ______________________________

B> ______________________________

B> ______________________________

B> ______________________________

B> ______________________________

Chapter 5 Answer Key

Compare your answers to the Self-Test with the correct answers given below. If all your answers are correct you are ready to go on to the next chapter. If you missed any questions, you may find it helpful to review the frames given in parentheses following the answer.

1. Your answer should include these points:
   - display device status
   - change device status

2. The system can't find the STAT.COM file on A disk.

3. a. A>STAT A:
   b. A>STAT B:=R/O
   c. A>STAT *.COM
   d. ^C
   e. A>STAT

4. Type any key

5. a. A>STAT PIP.COM $SYS
   b. A>STAT INVENTY.PRN $R/O
   c. A>STAT SORT.COM
   d. A>STAT USR:
   e. A>STAT DSK:
   f. A>STAT B:*.*
   g. A>STAT VAL:

6. B>STAT USR:

7. B>DIR
   B>USER 0
   B>DIR

8. (Optional.) You need to give all files read/write status before you can erase them. In our solution, we erase user 0 files then switch to user 1. The last step erases all remaining files.

```
B>STAT *.* $R/W
B>ERA *.*
B>USER 1
B>STAT *.* $R/W
B>ERA *.*
```

Suggested Machine Exercises

1. Start your system.
2. Boot. (Use a disk with STAT.COM.)
3. If you have a line printer, turn on echo print.

Steps 4-13 experiment with disk read/write status.

4. Install any disk in B drive but *don't reboot.*
5. Display the status of both disks. A should be R/W and B should be R/O.
6. Reboot (^C).
7. The reboot turned off echo print so turn it back on again.
8. Display the status of both disks again. Both should now be R/W.
9. Make the A disk R/O.
10. Display a directory of the A disk.
11. Try to erase one of the files on the A disk. (For safety's sake, choose a file that is duplicated on another disk.) What happens? You should get a BDOS error message. Do you remember what to do now? Type any character.
12. The reboot turned off echo print so turn it back on again.

Steps 13-15 experiment with the file status functions.

13. Display the status of STAT.COM.
14. Display the status of all COM files on the A disk.
15. Display the status of all files on the B disk.

The remaining steps pertain to release 2.0 and beyond. If you're working with an earlier release, skip the remaining steps and go on to chapter 6.

Steps 16-19 continue to experiment with the file status function.

16. Display a directory for your user number.

17. Select any file and make it a system file.

18. Display a new directory. Notice that your system file does not appear.

19. Restore the file to directory status.

Step 20 demonstrates the drive status function.

20. Display the characteristics of all disk drives on your system.

Steps 21-23 demonstrate the user status feature.

21. Display the current user status.

22. Change your user number.

23. Display the user status again.

This completes the suggested terminal practice for STAT. When you are ready, go on to chapter 6.

CHAPTER SIX

Using PIP

One of the most useful CP/M utility programs is the peripheral interchange program – PIP. PIP is used to transfer files from one device to another. You can copy a file from disk to disk, or from disk to a peripheral device such as CON: or LST:. You can also transfer files from an input device such as CON: or RDR: to any other device. Thus, PIP is one way to create a new disk file under CP/M. (You'll be learning the usual way in later chapters.) PIP can be used to copy the CP/M programs from one disk to another so you'll need PIP whenever you initialize a disk. You'll find you use PIP more and more as you become more familiar with it.

PIP can also combine files into a new file, and modify the file or files as it copies. In almost all cases, the original source file is unaffected by PIP; changes appear in the new file.

After you complete this chapter, you will be able to:

- Write a PIP command to copy a single file.
- Use the continuing PIP format to copy a series of files.
- Use generalized names to copy a collection of files using either PIP format.
- Use PIP parameters to specify changes in the new file(s).
- Use PIP to concatenate files.
- Place a copy of PIP.COM in a new user area.

1. The CP/M utility program that you use to copy files is called PIP – the peripheral interchange program. With PIP you can copy a file onto the same or another disk, changing its name if you wish. You can also combine files or copy several files with one command. By using codes you can modify the copied file, such as putting it in all upper case letters or adding line numbers.

Name the CP/M program that accomplishes each function below.

(a) Make a copy of a file on another disk. ____________

(b) Give the amount of space left on a disk. ____________

(c) Copy the system tracks to a new disk. ____________

(d) Copy a data file, convert it to lower case, and rename it. ______________

(a) PIP; (b) STAT; (c) SYSGEN; (d) PIP

2. In order to use PIP to copy files, the PIP.COM file must be present on an installed disk and available to your user number. Later in this chapter we'll see how to get PIP into your user area. A drive prefix can be used with PIP to access the program from any drive.

When you copy a file with PIP, the original file is not altered. It remains in the previous location after the PIP operation. Any requested changes will appear in the new version, which may have the same name if it is on a different disk or user or user number.

The general form of the basic PIP command is:

PIP destination-file=source-file [parameters]<CR>

Any changes to the file are specified as parameters. We'll cover those later in the chapter. First we'll examine the basic copy function of PIP.

(a) Suppose you have the PIP.COM file on drive A, but drive B is active. How can invoke PIP without switching the active drive? ______________

(b) Here is a valid PIP command:

A>PIP PROGRAM.FOR=SAMPLE.FOR

Which file(s) exist(s) before the PIP command is entered?

____

(c) Which file(s) exist(s) after the PIP program is executed?

____

(d) What difference will there be between the two files? ______________

____

(a) A:PIP; (b) SAMPLE.FOR; (c) PROGRAM.FOR and SAMPLE.FOR;
(d) just the name

3. A specific file can be copied to the same disk or to another. The drive name prefix can be part of either or both filenames in the PIP command. Whenever the drive name is omitted, the active drive is assumed for that file. For example, in this command:

A>B:PIP STOCK.MOD=B:STOCK.MED

____

PIP.COM is on drive B, as is the source file STOCK.MED. The destination file is to be created on drive A, the active drive. For each example below, give the drive on which the PIP program and the source file are located, and identify the drive where the destination file is to be created.

(a) B>A:PIP A:PAY.FOR=PAY.FOR

PIP ____________ source ____________ destination ____________

(b) A>PIP PAY.FOR=PAYROLL.FOR

PIP ____________ source ____________ destination ____________

(c) C>A:PIP B:PAY.COM=C:PAY.COM

PIP ____________ source ____________ destination ____________

(d) B>PIP A:PAY.DAT=B:PAY:PER

PIP ____________ source ____________ destination ____________

- - - - - - - - - - - - - - - -

(a) A, B, A; (b) A, A, A; (c) A, C, B; (d) B, B, A

4. Write commands to perform these operations. PIP.COM resides on the active disk.

(a) Copy a file named PEOPLE.DAT from drive A to drive B. Don't change the name.

A> ____

(b) Copy the same file as in (a), but change the name to EMPLOYEE.LST.

A> ____

(c) Copy file SALARY.HST from drive B to drive A. Don't change the name.

A> ____

(d) Make another copy of SALARY.HST on drive A. Name the new copy SALARY2.HST.

A> ____

- - - - - - - - - - - - - - - -

(a) A>PIP B:PEOPLE.DAT=PEOPLE.DAT (or =A:PEOPLE.DAT)
(b) A>PIP B:EMPLOYEE.LST=PEOPLE.DAT (or =A:PEOPLE.DAT)
(c) A>PIP SALARY.HST=B:SALARY.HST (or A:SALARY.HST=)
(d) A>PIP SALARY2.HST=SALARY.HST

5. Abbreviated PIP commands can be used when you are copying files without changing names. This may happen when you are copying from one disk to another or from one user number to another. You can use any of these forms:

PIP specific-filename=d:

PIP d1:specific-filename=d2:

PIP d:=filename

PIP d1:=d2:filename

Answer (a) in the preceding frame could be written PIP B:PEOPLE.DAT=A: or B:=PEOPLE.DAT and would have the same effect. Answer (c) could be written PIP A:=B:SALARY.HST or SALARY.HST=B: instead. The file named SALARY.HST on disk B would be copied to the A drive and given the same name.

Write the shortest possible commands to copy these files. PIP.COM is on disk A.

(a) Make a copy of file B:MONEY.XYZ on disk A. Change the name to MONEY. BAK.

A> ______________________________

(b) Copy the same file as in (a), but don't change the filename.

A> ______________________________

(c) Make a copy of file ANTHRO.REC from drive A onto drive B. Don't change the name.

A> ______________________________

- - - - - - - - - - - - - - - -

(a) A>PIP MONEY.BAK=B:MONEY.XYZ
(b) A>PIP MONEY.XYZ=B: or A:=B:MONEY.XYZ
(c) A>PIP B:ANTHRO.REC=A: or B:=A:ANTHRO.REC

6. We've been talking about copying one file at a time by specifying a specific filename in the PIP command. CP/M also lets you specify a general filename as a source file causing several files to be copied. The rules for coding general filenames for use in PIP are the same as those in other CP/M commands. You can use an * to fill out one part of the name with any characters, or a ? to fill a specific position with any character.

When you use a general filename the command must take this form:

PIP d:=general-filename
PIP d1:=d2:general-filename

The command PIP B:=*.COM will result in the copy of all files from the active disk that have filetype COM to disk B. No names are changed. If COM files already exist on disk B with the same names, they are destroyed. When you specify a general filename in a PIP command, PIP displays the specific names of the files it copies so you know the results.

Assume PIP is on disk A.

(a) Write a command to copy all files of filetype FOR from disk A to disk B.

A> ________________________________

(b) Write a command to copy all files from disk B to disk C.

A> ________________________________

(c) Write a command to copy all files whose filenames begin with A2 from disk B to disk A.

A> ________________________________

\- - - - - - - - - - - - - - - -

(a) PIP B:=*.FOR; (b) PIP C:=B:*.*; (c) PIP A:=B:A2*.*

7. PIP can also be used to combine several source files into a single destination file. This process is called *concatenation.* Here is the command format for concatenation:

PIP destination=source1,source2,source3,etc.

The destination filename is written as usual. The source filenames you wish to combine are typed and separated by commas. All the names must be specific; no ambiguity is allowed. Each source file is processed separately so each can be on a different disk if necessary. CP/M assumes each source file to be concatenated contains printable (ASCII) characters and ends with an end-of-file character (^Z). (You'll learn how to create this type of file in chapter 7.) The end-of-file characters, except for the last, are eliminated in the destination file.

(a) Write a command to combine files ONE.ASM and TWO.ASM into a new file, NEW.ASM, on the same drive.

A> ________________________________

(b) Write a command to combine these three files: STOCK.ONE, STOCK.TWO and STOCK,THR, from drive B into a file MASTER.STK on drive A.

A> ________________________________

(c) How many end-of-file marks will be in MASTER.STK after the three source files are concatenated? ____________________

\- - - - - - - - - - - - - - - -

(a) A>PIP NEW.ASM=ONE.ASM,TWO.ASM

(b) A>PIP MASTER.STK=B:STOCK.ONE,B:STOCK.TWO,B:STOCK.THR
(Did you put the drivename before each source filename? In this example, it's necessary or PIP will look on disk A for the file/s.)

(c) only one

8. When files are concatenated under CP/M, they are combined in the order you specify. If the destination file existed before the command, its data is replaced with the new file. The source files are unchanged in most cases, but it's possible to specify the destination as one of the source files. For example:

PIP MASTER.STK=MASTER.STK,STOCK.ADD

In this case, the files MASTER.STK and STOCK.ADD will be combined into a single file which will replace the original MASTER.STK.

(a) Write a command to combine files FIX.ONE from disk A, disk B, and disk C into a file FIX.ALL on disk B.

A> ________________________________

(b) Write a command to combine the three source files from (a) into the original source file from disk B.

B> ________________________________

(c) In which of the above cases [(a) or (b)] are the source files unchanged after the concatenation? ________________________

– – – – – – – – – – – – – – – –

(a) A>PIP B:FIX.ALL=FIX.ONE,B:FIX.ONE,C:FIX.ONE
(b) A>PIP B:FIX.ONE=FIX.ONE,B:FIX.ONE,C:FIX.ONE
(c) in (a)

9. PIP also allows you to refer to physical and logical devices that are attached to your system. The logical devices you can use are the ones given in STAT – CON: (console) and LST: (list) being the most common ones. Another useful device name is PRN: (print). PRN: is similar to LST:, except that under PRN: tabs are expanded to every eighth character position, lines are numbered, and a new page starts every 60 lines. Several additional device names are also available but aren't used much by non-programmers.

You can combine file and device names in the same PIP command. For example, PIP CON:=B:STUDENT.DAT will copy the file STUDENT.DAT from disk B to the console.

(a) Write a command to concatenate files A:FILE.ONE and B:FILE.TWO and copy them to the list device. Use line numbers, tab expansion, and paging.

A> ________________________________

(b) Perform the operation in (a) above but don't use line numbers, tab expansion, or paging.

A> ________________________________

(c) Copy file NEW.ASM from disk B to the console device.

A> ____

- - - - - - - - - - - - - - - -

(a) A>PIP PRN:=FILE.ONE,B:FILE.TWO;
(b) A>PIP LST:=FILE.ONE,B:FILE.TWO
(c) A>PIP CON:=B:NEW.ASM

10. When you enter a PIP command, CP/M copies the file. You may be able to hear disk movements or changes. When the operation is complete you'll receive the active drive prompt again.

If you enter a command that is invalid for some reason, you'll get an "INVALID FORMAT" or "NO FILE" message. The copy will not even begin if the command line is not correctly formed.

You can't interrupt or abort the PIP process once it has begun unless your destination is a device such as CON:, LST:, or PRN:. If so, you can interrupt the output using ^S, as usual, and restart it with any character except ^C. You can abort the command by typing any character except ^S. PIP responds with:

```
ABORTED: filename
A>_
```

What is indicated by each of these interactions?

(a)
```
A>PIP FIX.ONE=FIX.BAK

PIP?
A>_
```

____

(b)
```
A>PIP FIX.ONE=FIX.BAK

NO FILE: =FIX.BAK
A>_
```

____

(c)
```
A>PIP FIX.ONE,FIX.BAK

INVALID FORMAT: ,

A>_
```

____

____

(d)
```
A>PIP LST:=FIX.BAK

ABORTED: FIX.BAK

A> _
```

(a) PIP.COM is not on disk A; (b) file FIX.BAK is not on disk A;
(c) we need = instead of , ; (d) the PIP operation was aborted

11. We have been discussing the one-line command format of PIP. All of the functions and formats we've covered also work with the other PIP format. If you simply enter PIP and press carriage return, PIP responds with a PIP command prompt like this:

```
A>PIP
*_
```

Now you can enter a command line, just as in a one-line PIP command. When you enter the line, the operation takes place. However, instead of returning you to CP/M at the active drive, the system leaves you in PIP and gives you another command prompt. You can continue entering command lines until you don't need PIP anymore. To return to CP/M level simply press carriage return when you receive an asterisk (*). You are immediately returned to the active drive.

Suppose you need to copy three files FIX.ONE, FOX.TWO, and FOX.TWI from disk A to disk B. You also need a file B:FOXY.ALL made up of FOX.TWO and FOX.TWI. You'll want to use the multiple line format.

(a) Write your first entry.

A> ________________________________

(b) Write a command line to copy FIX.ONE

* ________________________________

(c) Write a command line to copy FOX.TWO and FOX.TWI

* ________________________________

(d) Write a command line to create B:FOXY.ALL

* ________________________________

(e) How do you terminate PIP?

* ________________________________

(a) A>PIP; (b) *B:=FIX.ONE; (c) *B:=FOX.TW?;
(d) *B:FOXY.ALL=FOX.TWO,FOX.TWI; (e) carriage return
(In (d) you could have used the source files on disk B.)

12. The multiple line format of PIP may also be used to copy files on disks that don't contain PIP.COM. For example, suppose you have disk 1 containing PIP.COM and disk 2 containing SORT.COM. You want to copy SORT.COM to disk 3, which doesn't contain PIP.COM either. Also, suppose you have only two drives.

First, put disk 1 on drive A, disk 3 on drive B, and enter PIP. CP/M responds:

```
A>PIP
*_
```

Then remove disk 1 from drive A, install disk 2, and enter:

```
*B:=SORT.COM
```

The copy will be successfully made.

After starting PIP, you cannot write on the disk you changed. (It will have R/O status.)

Suppose you also want to copy SORT.MSG to disk 3. However, it's on disk 4, which does not contain PIP. If the above PIP session is ongoing, how would you make the copy?

Put disk 4 in drive A and enter *B:=SORT.MSG.

You have now seen the basic copy functions of PIP. With PIP you can copy one file with a specific filename, or several files with an ambigious name. You've seen how to concatenate files with PIP and how to use both PIP formats. Now we're going to look at the PIP parameters. Each of these has a specific effect on the copy operation.

The PIP command has 19 different parameters that you can use to modify the file being copied. Appendix B includes a complete listing with brief explanations for you to refer to later. We're going to look at the various parameters and see how you can use them as you work with CP/M.

13. One useful parameter is E, which stands for "echo." When you use the E parameter the transferred data is also echoed (or displayed) on the console. This tends to slow down the PIP operation, however it does show exactly what is being transferred. To use a parameter, enclose it in square brackets [E] immediately following the source filename.

Which of these commands is correctly formed?

_____ (a) PIP [E]STOK.ONE=STOK.TWO

_____ (b) PIP STOK.ONE[E]=STOK.TWO

_____ (c) PIP STOK.ONE=STOK.TWO[E]

- - - - - - - - - - - - - - - -

(c)

14. Parameters are available for translating a file into all upper case letters (U) or all lower case (L). The destination file will be all one case or the other, depending on the parameter used. Parameters can be combined as in this example:

PIP STOK.ONE=STOK.TWO[EU]

The file STOK.TWO will be transferred as STOK.ONE, with all lower case letters converted to upper case. STOK.ONE will be echoed on the console. The parameters can be in any order and either upper case or lower case letters may be used.

Write commands with parameters to accomplish these operations.

(a) Copy FILE.X from disk A to disk B. Convert all upper case letters to lower case. Don't display it on the console.

A> _____

(b) Copy all files of type SM6 from disk B to disk A. Convert lower case letters to upper case. Don't display any on the console.

A> _____

(c) Copy file DEPART.TYM as DEPART.NEW. Convert to all upper case letters and display the transferred data.

A> _____

- - - - - - - - - - - - - - - -

(a) PIP B:=A:FILE.X[L] ; (b) PIP A:=B:*.SM6[U] ;
(c) PIP DEPART.NEW=DEPART.TYM[UE] or [EU]

15. Some parameters can be used only with certain types of files. Only files with alphabetic characters, for example, can be converted to upper case or lower case. And only printable characters will make sense on the console. The Dn parameter – delete n characters – only makes sense for certain files. When you specify Dn, any characters that extend beyond column *n* are deleted. This can only be done with a file containing printable characters. Dn is often used to truncate long lines that are being sent to a narrow printer or console. If a print device has only 40 columns, you might specify [D40], especially if you only need to see the first 40 columns.

(a) Could you specify D60 for a COM file? ______________________

(b) Write a command to transfer FILE.XY as FILE.AB, convert it to upper case, delete anything beyond column 50, and echo the result on the console.

A> ______________________

- - - - - - - - - - - - - - - -

(a) no – COM files aren't printable files;

(b) PIP FILE.AB=FILE.XY[UED50] (The parameters can be in any order.)

16. You saw earlier that you can PIP a file to the PRN: device with the result that line numbers are added, tabs are expanded, and a page break occurs every 60 lines. With three parameters you can achieve the same effect on a LST: or disk file. If you then TYPE the resulting disk file, the effect will be the same as PIPping it directly to PRN:, but now you also have a copy on disk. Here are the parameters:

N	Add line numbers
Tn	Expand tabs every *n* columns
Pn	Start a new page every *n* lines

If you use T without *n*, no tabs are expanded. If you use P without *n*, a page break occurs every 60 lines. Therefore a parameter of [NT8P] or [NT8P60] has the same effect as PIPping a file to the PRN: device.

Write parameter lists to accomplish the following:

(a) Convert to lower case, expand tabs to every 4th column.

____

(b) Page after 50 lines, add line numbers, and limit destination file to 80 characters per line.

____

(c) Create a disk file in the same format as a PRN: file.

____

- - - - - - - - - - - - - - - -

(a) [LT4] ; (b) [NP50D80] ; (c) [NT8P] or [NT8P60]

17. When line numbers are added with [N], leading zeros are suppressed and the number is followed by a colon, like this.

```
1: LINE1
2: LINE2
```

____

If you specify [N2], leading zeros are printed and a tab is inserted following the number. If the destination is disk, T8 is assumed. If the destination is LST:, the tab setting on the printer is used. In the example below we had the printer tab set at 15.

```
000001          LINE1
000002          LINE2
```

If you specify [N2Tn], the tabs will be expanded so that the next character begins in column n+1. For [N2T10] the display looks like this:

```
000001    LINE1
000002    LINE2
```

Don't use E with N. The combination is legal but the line numbers get mixed up because PIP numbers the lines that are displayed as well as the lines that are stored or listed.

(a) Write the parameter list to number lines in this format:

```
1:   RESTORE1
2:   RESTORE2
```

* ____________________

(b) Write the parameter list to number the lines and insert tabs, expanded to column 15.____________________

\- - - - - - - - - - - - - - - -

(a) [N] ; (b) [N2T14]

18. The F parameter is used to filter, or remove, form feeds (page breaks) from a file. Suppose you created a disk file using this parameter list [NT8P50]. Now you want to print it out but you need exactly 54 lines per page. What do you do? You use this command:

PIP LST:=CURRENT.FIL[FP54]

The F parameter filters all the page breaks from CURRENT.FIL and P54 inserts new ones every 54 lines. If F and P are in the same parameter list, the existing page breaks are always removed before the new ones are added.

Assume that DOCUMENT.FUL was originally created with these parameters: [N2T8P60]. Write commands to accomplish the following:

(a) Print DOCUMENT.FUL with line numbers, tabs expanded normally, and 60 lines per page.

A> ____________________

(b) Print DOCUMENT.FUL with tabs expanded every 10 columns and 48 lines per page.

A> ______________________________

(c) Print DOCUMENT.FUL with tabs expanded every eight columns and no page breaks.

A> ______________________________

- - - - - - - - - - - - - - - -

(a) TYPE DOCUMENT.FUL (or PIP LST:=DOCUMENT.FUL);

(b) PIP LST:=DOCUMENT.FUL[FP48T10] ; (c) PIP LST:=DOCUMENT.FUL[F]

(Remember that the order of parameters and whether you use capital or small letters is unimportant. You may use parameters that would occur anyway, such as T8 for question (c) above.)

19. We've covered quite a few PIP parameters for use with files that contain character data. Before we continue, give the parameter you'd use to accomplish each of these functions:

______ (a) Display transferred data on the console.

______ (b) Expand tabs every six columns.

______ (c) Insert a page break every 50 lines.

______ (d) Remove all page breaks.

______ (e) Convert lower case letters to upper case.

______ (f) Convert upper case letters to lower case.

______ (g) Add line numbers to a file.

______ (h) PIP only the first 72 characters of each line.

- - - - - - - - - - - - - - - -

(a) E; (b) T6; (c) P50; (d) F; (e) U; (f) L; (g) N or N2; (h) D72

20. Sometimes you may not want to copy an entire file in a PIP operation. You can use the S and Q parameters to tell PIP to start (S) and quit (Q) copying at certain points. If you use S, but not Q, the copy will start at the point you specify and run to the end of file. If you use Q, but not S, the copy will start at the beginning of the file and quit where you specify. If you use both, you can determine both the first and last parts of the new file.

You specify the starting or quitting location as a string of characters. Suppose you want to start copying where the word SUBROUTINE first appears. You code the parameter like this:

[SSUBROUTINE^Z]

To quit where the next RETURN appears, you'd modify the parameter to look like this:

[SSUBROUTINE^ZQRETURN^Z]

Notice that each string is terminated with ^Z. Upper and lower case letters in the string must exactly match in the file.

Write parameters to indicate the following:

(a) Begin the copy operation where CHAPTER 2 occurs.

____

(b) The last part of the new file should be ;END.

____

(c) Assume the text of this frame is a file. You want a copy the third sentence into a separate file.

____

- - - - - - - - - - - - - - - -

(a) [SCHAPTER 2^Z]; (b) [Q;END^Z]; (c) [SIf you^ZQfile.^Z]

21. You might have coded more words for question (c) of the preceding frame. That's perfectly all right. The copy will start at the first "If you" and end after the next "file." it encounters.

The S and Q strings are converted to upper case in the one-line PIP format, just as parameters and commands are in CP/M. So whenever you are dealing with upper and lower case, as in that example, you need to use the continuing PIP format.

The spacing, punctuation, and capitalization must be exact for PIP to identify a string.

Suppose you want to PIP a file to contain the second paragraph of this frame. Which of the following will accomplish that?

_____ (a) A>PIP LINES.45=FRAME.20[SThe S^ZQcontinuing PIP format.^Z]

_____ (b) A>PIP
*LINES.45=FRAME.20[SThe S^ZQPIP format^Z]

_____ (c) A>PIP
*LINES.45=FRAME.20[SThe S^ZQcontinuing PIP format.^Z]

- - - - - - - - - - - - - - - -

(c) (The strings in (a) would be converted to upper case and wouldn't match. (b) would copy only the first part of the first sentence.)

22. When you are working on version 2 CP/M you may want to copy a file from another user area to the active one. You do this with the Gn parameter where *n* specifies the user number of the source file. If you are working under user 3, for example, and have PIP.COM under user 3, you can copy files from other user areas. You might use PIP STAT.COM=STAT.COM[G0] to copy the STAT program from user area 0 into your area. If STAT is a system file under user 0, you also need to specify parameter R. Then STAT will be a system file after it is copied as well. These parameters (G and R) are not available before version 2 of CP/M, since user numbers and system files aren't used then.

Assume you are under user number 5 and you have PIP in your area. Write commands to accomplish the following:

(a) Copy the file ASM.COM from user area 1 to user area 5.

A> ____

(b) Copy all non-system files from user area 0 to user area 4.

A> ____

A> ____

(c) Copy all files, including system files from user area 4 to user area 5.

A> ____

A> ____

- - - - - - - - - - - - - - - -

(a) A>PIP A:=ASM.COM[G1]

(b) A>USER 4
A>PIP A:=*.*[G0]

(c) A>USER 5
A>PIP A:=*.*[G4R]

23. Under normal conditions PIP will not overlay a file that is set to R/O status. If you attempt this, CP/M tells you:

DESTINATION FILE IS R/O. DELETE (Y/N)?

If you enter Y, the file will be overlaid with the copied file of the same name. If you make any other response, the file is not transferred and CP/M says **NOT DELETED**. If you want PIP to go ahead and overlay without asking you each time, you can use the W parameter. Any R/O files will be deleted and replaced with new ones. Like G and R, W is available only in version 2.0 and later.

Consider this command:

A>PIP A:*.*[G3RW]

(a) What is the general effect? ______________________________

____

(b) Suppose you are user 1 and the only file in your area is PIP.COM, which is set to R/O. If user area 3 contains PIP.COM as a system file, will it be transferred?

__________ Will your PIP.COM be overlaid? __________

(c) How could you modify the command above so that the system files will be copied from user area 3, but CP/M will ask before overlaying any R/O files?

____

- - - - - - - - - - - - - - - -

(a) copy all files from user area 3 to the active area; (b) yes, yes;
(c) PIP A:*.*[G3R] (eliminate the W)

Several PIP parameters are used only in special cases: B, O, H, I, and Z. We won't cover them in this book. Another parameter [V] can be used with all PIP operations, but it tends to double the time PIP takes. When you specify [V], the PIP operation is verified before CP/M returns you to command level. If you will be writing your own programs, or using non-ASCII files, you may want to look these additional parameters up in Appendix B.

24. Write PIP commands with parameters required to accomplish the following:

(a) Copy file RILEY.WIL to the list device. Number each line, expand tabs to every fifth position, change the page breaks to every 70 lines.

A> ____

(b) Print the portion of RILEY.WIL that begins "To my son" and ends "Washington, D.C.". These must not be interpreted as upper case. Use the PRN: device.

A> ____

* ____

(c) How do you return control to the active drive?

____

- - - - - - - - - - - - - - - -

(a) PIP LST:=RILEY.WIL[NT5FP70]

(b) PIP
*PRN:=RILEY.WIL[STo my son^ZQWashington, D.C.^Z]

(c) carriage return

25. We can use PIP to copy files from one user area to another. How do we get the PIP.COM file into a user area (other than 0) to start with? You can't use PIP to move it because PIP isn't there. The solution to this dilemma lies in forcing PIP.COM into the TPA and then using the SAVE command to store it. Examine the following interaction. User 0 is active at the beginning and PIP.COM is available under user 0.

```
(1)  A>PIP
     *<CR>

     A>USER 3
(2)  A>SAVE 32 PIP.COM
     A>_
```

(a) What is the effect of command (1) ?

____

(b) What is the effect of command (2) ?

____

(c) Write the commands needed to store PIP under user 2. Start from user 0 and assume that you've just booted and the TPA is empty.

____

____

____

____

____

- - - - - - - - - - - - - - -

(a) PIP is *loaded into the TPA* and given control; (b) the first 32 pages of the TPA (which currently contain the PIP program) are stored as PIP.COM under user 3.

(c)
```
A>PIP
*<CR>

A>USER 2

A>SAVE 32 PIP.COM
A>_
```

26. At the time of this writing, our version of PIP takes 32 pages. However the size may change. Therefore you should find out how many pages you need to save for your version of PIP.

Here's how you can find out. STAT PIP.COM will show you the number of bytes in PIP, thus:

```
A>STAT PIP.COM
RECS  BYTES  EXT  ACC
  58     8K    1  R/W A:PIP.COM
```

____

Save four pages for every 1K bytes. (A page is 256 bytes, and 1K is 1024 bytes.)

Suppose STAT PIP.COM shows this result:

```
RECS  BYTES  EXT  ACC
  65     9K    1  R/W  A:PIP.COM
```

Show the commands to move PIP from user area 0 to user area 4.

____

____

____

____

____

____

- - - - - - - - - - - - - - -

```
A>PIP
*<CR>

A>USER 4

A>SAVE 36 PIP.COM
A>_
```

CHAPTER 6 SELF-TEST

1. Write the command to copy CHAP6.EX to the same disk under the name CHAP6.TST. A> ______________________

2. Write the command to copy CHAP6.EX from disk A to disk B. Keep the same name. A> ______________________

3. Write the command to copy all files from disk A to disk B.

   A> ______________________

4. Write the command to copy all files starting with the characters 'CHAP6' from disk B to disk A.

   A> ______________________

5. Write the command to combine CHAP6.P1 and CHAP6.P2 as CHAP6.PRN. All three files are on disk A.

   A> ______________________

6. Write the command to combine CHAP6 from disk B with CH6.TST and CH6.EX from disk A. The new file should replace CHAP6 on disk B. Echo the transferred data on the console.

   A> ______________________________

7. Write the command to display CHAP6.PRN on the console, translating all letters to lower case.

   A> ______________________________

8. Write the command to print CHAP6.PRN on the line printer with line numbers, tabs expanded to the eighth column, and page breaks every 60 lines.

   A> ______________________________

9. Write the command to print CHAP6.PRN on the line printer, with line numbers. Delete everything after column 40.

   A> ______________________________

10. Write the commands to print CHAP6.PRN on the console, from "1." through "concatenation."

    A> ______________________________

    * ______________________________

11. Write the command to print CHAP6.PRN on the line printer, remove the existing form feeds, and change pages every 45 lines.

    A> ______________________________

12. Write the command to copy CHAP6.PRN from user 0 to user 3. Assume that you are starting as user 0.

    A> ______________________________

    A> ______________________________

13. Write the command to copy all files, including system files, from user 0 to user 3. Don't overlay any existing files if they have R/O status.

    A> ______________________________

14. Change your command from question 13 so that existing R/O files are overlaid.

    A> ______________________________

15. Starting from user 0, write the commands to copy PIP.COM to user 4.

Chapter 6 Answer Key

1. A>PIP CHAP6.TST=CHAP6.EX

2. A>PIP B:=CHAP6.EX

3. A>PIP B:=*.*

4. A>PIP A:=B:CHAP6*.*

5. A>PIP CHAP6.PRN=CHAP6.P1,CHAP6.P2

6. A>PIP B:CHAP6=B:CHAP6,CH6.TST,CH6.EX[E]

7. A>PIP CON:=CHAP6.PRN[L]

8. A>PIP PRN:=CHAP6.PRN

9. A>PIP LST:=CHAP6.PRN[ND40]

10. A>PIP
*CON:=CHAP6.PRN[S1.^ZQconcatenation.^Z]

11. A>PIP LST:=CHAP6.PRN[FP45]

12. A>USER 3
    A>PIP A:=CHAP6.PRN [GO]

13. A>PIP A:=*.* [GOR]

14. A>PIP A:=*.* [GORW]

15. A>PIP
    *<CR>
    A>USER 4
    A>SAVE 32 PIP.COM

Suggested Machine Exercises

1. Start up your system and boot from a disk containing PIP.COM and plenty of extra space.
2. Get a disk directory and select a file to be copied. Don't choose a COM or HEX file. You might use STAT to help you select a short one.
3. PIP the file to TRY.1 on the same disk.
4. Check the disk directory for TRY.1.
5. PIP the file to TRY.2 (same disk) and have it echo on the console.
6. PIP the file to TRY.3 using line numbering and tabs every 10th column.
7. TYPE TRY.3 to see the effect.
8. If you're running out of disk space, erase TRY.1, TRY.2, and TRY.3.
9. PIP the file to TRY.4 using lower case translation. Use echo to see the effect.

Try using the multiple line format for the next three commands.

10. PIP the file to the console.
11. PIP the file to PRN:.
12. PIP the file to LST: and compare the results.
13. Try making two new files, TRY.5 and TRY.6, from parts of the source file. Use echo to see the effect.
14. Concatenate TRY.5 and TRY.6 into TRY.7. TYPE TRY.7 to see the effect.
15. Try some faulty commands. How about PIP A:=TRY.9. Or try PIP A: = TRY.6.

If you only have one disk drive, skip steps 16-18.

16. Install a disk on drive B and reboot.

17. PIP TRY.7 from A to B.

18. PIP TRY.7 from B to A.

If you don't have CP/M version 2.0 or later, skip steps 19-20.

19. Transfer PIP.COM to a different user number on the A disk.

20. PIP TRY.7 from user 0 to the new number.

21. Just for fun, use PIP to create a file.

    a. Enter PIP JUNK.FIL=CON:.

    b. The cursor will more to the next line. Type a few words.

    c. Hit <CR>. You may need to depress the line feed key as well.

    d. Type another line.

    e. Enter ^Z.

22. Use the TYPE command to see your file (TYPE JUNK.FIL).

23. Erase all the various files you have created in this exercise.

Now go on to Chapter 7.

CHAPTER SEVEN

Introduction to ED

The ED program is the CP/M text editor. You use ED to type new files and store them on disk. You also use ED to change existing files.

ED is different from the other CP/M programs you have studied. When you enter d>ED filename, you go to the ED command level. You can then enter a wide variety of ED commands. You interact with ED in the same fashion that you interact with the CCP. In this chapter, and the following two, you will learn the ED commands and how to use them.

In Chapter 7 you'll learn how to initiate ED. You'll study some general ED facilities such as line numbering. Then you'll learn how to create a new text file under ED and how to save that file on disk. In your Suggested Machine Exercises you'll actually create a new file.

When you have finished this chapter, you will be able to:

- Initiate ED for a new file.
- Turn line numbering on and off.
- Turn upper case translation on and off.
- Initiate ED's insert level.
- Type and store data in memory.
- Use the CP/M control characters under ED.
- Terminate insert level.
- Terminate ED.
- State the meaning of various ED messages.

1. ED is a text editor. You use it to create and change text files. ED is not used with binary or hexadecimal files such as COM or HEX files.

To create a file you type it on your console. ED stores it in the TPA and then, when you're ready, stores it on the disk.

To change a file, ED moves the file from disk into the TPA. You can then use editing commands to delete, insert, and/or replace data. When you're ready, ED stores the changed file back on the disk again. ED also keeps a backup copy of the original file, just in case you change your mind.

Which of the following can ED be used for?

______ (a) Create a new COM file.

______ (b) Create a new data file.

______ (c) Change an existing HEX file.

______ (d) Change an existing data file.

______ (e) Change the system tracks.

- - - - - - - - - - - - - - - -

(b) and (d) (We didn't discuss e, but by now you should know that you can only access the system tracks with SYSGEN and MOVCPM.)

CHARACTER EDITING

2. ED is a *character editor*. This means that you work on one character at a time. Characters are grouped together to form *lines*. To ED, a line is any string of characters terminated by carriage return and line feed characters. Both the carriage return and the line feed, in that order, must be present to mark the end of an ED line.

In this book we'll abbreviate carriage return as <CR> and line feed as <LF>.

When you're creating a new file with ED, type a line at your terminal, then hit <CR>. ED stores the <CR> character and *automatically adds a <LF> character.* Both the <CR> and <LF> are displayed on your terminal. You won't see "<CR> <LF>". You'll see the effect – the cursor moves to the beginning of a new line.

(a) What is a line?

______ 80 characters on the console.

______ Any string of data in memory terminated by <CR>.

______ Any string of data in memory terminated by <CR> <LF>.

(b) According to the above definition, could a line contain zero characters? ______

(c) Could it contain 6000 characters? ______

(d) When you're typing data under ED, how do you mark the end of a line?

______

(e) When you type <CR>, what does ED store in memory? ______

______

(f) What will be displayed on your console? ______________________

____

- - - - - - - - - - - - - - - -

(a) any string of data in memory terminated by <CR> <LF>; (b) yes; (c) yes (but it may look funny when displayed on your terminal or printed on your line printer); (d) type <CR>; (e) <CR> <LF>; (f) the cursor moves to the beginning of the next line

3. Suppose you're working with ED, and main memory contains this data:

```
THE ACME INSURANCE CORPORATION<CR><LF>CORDIALLY
INVITES YOU TO ATTEND A<CR><LF>NON-SMOKER'S SEMINAR
<CR><LF>DOWNTOWN PLAZA HOTEL<CR><LF>FEB. 4 AT 6 PM
<CR><LF><CR><LF>R.S.V.P.<CR><LF>
```

This file contains seven lines. The next to the last line is empty – it contains no data.

Now let's store this file on the disk and display it using TYPE. The display will look like this:

```
THE ACME INSURANCE CORPORATION
CORDIALLY INVITES YOU TO ATTEND A
NON-SMOKER'S SEMINAR
DOWNTOWN PLAZA HOTEL
FEB. 4 AT 6 PM

R.S.V.P.
```

Suppose you're working with ED and main memory contains this data:

```
NAME:<CR><LF>ADDRESS:<CR><LF><CR><LF>
<CR><LF>PHONE:<CR><LF>
```

(a) How many lines does this file contain? ______________________

(b) If you TYPE it out, what will it look like?

- - - - - - - - - - - - - - - -

(a) five;

(b)
```
NAME:
ADDRESS:


PHONE:
```

THE CHARACTER POINTER

4. As you fill memory with text data, ED keeps track of your position in memory. Imagine that ED maintains a pointer that always indicates your current position in memory. We call this the *character pointer* and show it like this:

```
THE ACME INSURANCE COMPANY<CR><LF>
                                  ^
```

The mark (^) indicates the character pointer. In our example it's at the beginning of a new line.

The location of the character pointer is very important. All the ED commands operate on the current character or the current line. For example, if you enter the command:

```
*D
```

ED will delete the character after the pointer. If you enter the command:

```
*-D
```

ED will delete the character before the pointer.

If you enter the command:

```
*K
```

ED will delete (Kill) the data from the character pointer to the end of the line.

Suppose main memory looks like this:

```
3142D NO. 2 PENCILS BOX/12<CR><LF>
                          ^
```

(a) Where is the character pointer?

______ at the end of the line

______ at the beginning of the next line

______ at the beginning of this line

(b) Suppose you enter this command:

```
*-D
```

What will the line look like in memory?

```
______ 3142D NO. 2 PENCILS BOX/12<LF>
                                 ^
______ 3142D NO. 2 PENCILS BOX/1<CR><LF>
                                ^
______ <CR><LF>
       ^
```

______ no change to line

(c) Suppose you enter this command:

*–K

What do you suppose the line will look like in memory?

______ 3142D NO. 2 PENCILS BOX/12^<LF>

______ 3142D NO. 2 PENCILS BOX/1^<CR><LF>

______ ^<CR><LF>

______ no change to line

- - - - - - - - - - - - - - - -

(a) at the end of the line; (b) 3142D NO. 2 PENCILS BOX/1^<CR><LF> ;
(c) ^<CR><LF>

5. ED includes a set of commands to move the character pointer wherever you want. You can move it forward or backward, by character or by line. You can also jump it to the beginning or end of the file in memory. There are also commands to display the current line so you can see exactly where the character pointer is. You'll be learning how to use all these commands in a later chapter, when you learn how to change an existing file.

For now, let's review what you've learned about character editing and the character pointer.

```
FOURSCORE AND SEVEN YEARS AGO<CR><LF>OUR FATHERS
BROUGHT FORTH ON THIS CONTINENT<CR><LF>^A NEW NA
TION CONCEIVED IN LIBERTY<CR><LF>
```

(a) How many lines are in the above example? ______

(b) Where is the character pointer? ______

(c) If you entered this command:

*D

What effect would it have?

______

(d) If you entered this command:

*K

What effect would it have?

______

- - - - - - - - - - - - - - - -

(a) 3; (b) at the beginning of the third line; (c) the "A" would be deleted;
(d) the third line would be killed

LINE NUMBERING

6. As a further aid in keeping track of lines, you can use ED's line numbering facility. If you want, ED will display a five-digit number at the beginning of each line on your console.

The line numbers are not stored with your data in memory. They just appear on the console when you display lines.

A typical display might look like this:

```
00001: PAUL JONES
00002: 16 MAPLE ST.
00003: POWAY, CA 92064
```

Which of the following statements are true?

______ (a) Line numbers are always displayed.

______ (b) Line numbering is optional.

______ (c) Line numbers are stored with the data in the file.

______ (d) Line numbers are displayed but not stored.

- - - - - - - - - - - - - - - -

(b) and (d)

7. Line numbering is turned on by the command:

*V

It's turned off by the command:

*–V

Line numbering was not available before version 1.4 of CP/M. In version 1.4, line numbering is automatically off when you initiate ED. To turn it on, you must use the V command.

With version 2.0 and later versions, line numbering is automatically on when you initiate ED. If you don't want to use the numbers you have to turn them off with the –V command.

(a) Show the ED command to turn line numbering on. * ________________

(b) Show the ED command to turn line numbering off. * ________________

(c) With your version of CP/M, will line numbering be on or off when you initiate ED? ________________________________

- - - - - - - - - - - - - - - -

(a) *V; (b) *–V; (c) the correct answer depends on the version of CP/M you're using

UPPER CASE TRANSLATION

Another ED facility is upper case translation. In the frames that follow, we'll show you what this is and how to use it.

8. Upper case translation means that all letters are stored as upper case letters, even if you type them as lower case letters. Numbers and other characters are not translated.

You may want to use this facility if your console allows you to type in either lower or upper case. If your console does not include lower case letters, you don't need to bother with upper case translation. But read on; you may get a new console next year.

Frequently, you want to type in all capital letters. On a regular typewriter you push the shift lock key. This has its disadvantages. Suppose you want to type this sentence:

THERE WERE 435 SUCH INCIDENTS IN 1980.

You have to shift lock, type THERE WERE, release the shift lock, type 435, shift lock again, type SUCH INCIDENTS IN, release the shift lock again, and type 1980. This is a clumsy, slow, and error-prone process.

If you use upper case translation instead, you leave the keyboard in lower case. Type the sentence as is and it will come out with the letters in upper case and the numbers in lower case – just what you wanted.

With upper case translation on, which of the following characters would be translated to upper case?

______ (a) ;	______ (d) f
______ (b) 5	______ (e) ,
______ (c) a	______ (f) x

– – – – – – – – – – – – – – – –

(c), (d), and (f)

9. If your console has both lower and upper case, it probably has an upper case translation feature built into the hardware. You will have a control button labeled U/C, UPPER, or something similar. With the button down, each letter that you type is translated by your console before it's sent. It will appear on your display in upper case.

If you choose to use ED's upper case translation feature instead, leave the UPPER CASE button up. Enter the ED command:

```
*U
```

ED will translate letters *after* they're sent. On your display you'll see the lower case letters. In memory, the upper case letters are stored. When you print or display the file, the capital letters will appear.

To turn upper case translation off again, enter:

*–U

(a) What's the ED command to turn on upper case translation? *______________

(b) What's the ED command to turn off upper case translation? *______________

– – – – – – – – – – – – – – – –

(a) *U; (b) *–U

Now that you have learned about character editing, the character pointer, line numbering, and upper case translation, you're ready to begin learning how to use ED. In this chapter we'll show you how to create a new file using ED. In later chapters we'll show you how to edit existing files.

THE SETUP

10. In order to create a new file, you're going to need two basic things: the ED.COM file and some available disk space for the new file. In this chapter we'll assume that both files will be on the same disk.

Suppose that a STAT of disk A shows that ED.COM is a system file with R/O status. There are 7K bytes left on A.

(a) Can you use the ED program to create a new file on this disk? ______________

(b) Suppose you plan to create a file containing 10K bytes. Can you do it on this disk? ____

– – – – – – – – – – – – – – – –

(a) yes; (b) no, you'll need a disk with more available space

11. Let's assume you want to build a file named MAILIST.DOC on the active disk, under user 0.

To assign MAILIST.DOC to user number 0, you must create it under user number 0. Therefore, you must have ED available under user number 0.

Suppose you're logged on as user 0. What's the best way to find out if ED.COM is on the disk for user 0?

______ (a) STAT ED.COM

______ (b) DIR ED.COM

– – – – – – – – – – – – – – – –

(a) is better if STAT is on the disk because if ED has system status it won't show up on DIR

12. The command to call ED and name the file is:

d>ED d:specific-filename

For our file, we would enter:

A>ED MAILIST.DOC

The ED program is loaded into the TPA and given control. It searches the disk directory for the filename. If found, it assumes you want to change the file. If not found, it assumes you want to create the file and it opens up two new directory entries on the disk. One directory entry is for the specific filename and the other is for a temporary work file named filename.$$$. ED will later erase the $$$ file.

(a) Suppose you want to create a file on A disk named INDEX.DAT. Show the command you would enter. A> ____________________

(b) Suppose ED.COM is on A disk but you want to create the file on B disk. Show the command you would enter. A>____________________

(c) How many directory entries must be available on a disk to create a new file with ED? ____________________

(d) After you enter the command in (a) above, what new files will ED put on A disk? Name the files. ____________________

(e) Can you use a generalized filename with ED? ____________________

- - - - - - - - - - - - - - - - -

(a) A>ED INDEX.DAT; (b) A>ED B:INDEX.DAT or A>B: followed by B>A:ED INDEX.DAT; (c) 2; (d) INDEX.DAT and INDEX.$$$; (e) no

13. When we enter A>ED MAILIST.DOC, we want the response shown below:

```
NEW FILE
     : *_
```

The first line tells us that we have given a filename that does not appear in the directory. Therefore, it's a new file.

The second line gives the line number, then gives the ED command prompt, *. The line number indicates the current location of the character pointer. When it's blank, the character pointer is at the beginning of a nonexistent line.

Earlier CP/M versions do not automatically include line numbering. The response looks like this:

```
NEW FILE
*_
```

(a) What is the ED command prompt? ____________________

____

(b) When you initiate ED, how can you tell whether line numbering is on or off?

____

(c) In the transaction below, show the command to turn line numbering off.

```
A>ED MAILIST.DOC
NEW FILE
     : *________
```

- - - - - - - - - - - - - - - -

(a) an asterisk (*); (b) whether a blank line number (:) appears before the prompt; (c) *–V

14. It's usually pretty simple to get ED started on a new file, but there are some things that can go wrong.

If ED isn't available, you'll get this message:

```
ED?

A>_
```

If the selected disk has read/only status, you'll get this message:

```
BDOS ERR ON A: R/O_
```

If the file already exists, a number of different things could happen. If the file has R/W and DIR status, ED assumes you want to change the file and gives this response:

```
A>ED INDEX.DOC
     : *_
```

When you see this response, you know that ED has found a file with the name you gave. In earlier versions it looks like this:

```
A>ED INDEX.DOC
*_
```

If the existing file has system status, you'll get this response:

```
A>ED INDEX.DOC
"SYSTEM" FILE NOT ACCESSIBLE

A>_
```

If the existing file has R/O status, you'll get this response:

```
** FILE IS READ/ONLY **
     : *_
```

This warning message tells you that you can read the file under ED, but you can't make any changes to it.

Suppose you want to create a new file named PRACTICE.DOC. You have this display:

```
A>ED PRACTICE.DOC

** FILE IS READ/ONLY **
     : *_
```

(a) What program level are you now at – CP/M or ED? ____________

(b) Can you now begin typing your new file? ________ Why or why not?

____

(c) How can you get out of this situation? ____________

____

Suppose instead you have this display.

```
A>ED PRACTICE.DOC
     : *_
```

(d) What program level are you now at – CP/M or ED? ____________

(e) Can you now begin typing your new file? ________ Why or why not?

____

Suppose you try to put your new file on B disk and get this response:

```
A>ED B:PRACTICE.DOC
BDOS ERROR ON B: R/O
```

(f) What's wrong? ____________

____

(g) How can you get out of this situation? ____________

____

____

____

- - - - - - - - - - - - - - - -

(a) ED; (b) no; there already is a PRACTICE.DOC file on the A disk; (c) one way is to use ^C to reboot, then start over using another filename; (d) ED; (e) no; the response indicates that there already is a PRACTICE.DOC file on a A disk because ED didn't say NEW FILE; (f) B disk has read/only status so ED can't open up a new directory entry; (g) type any key to reboot and then B disk will have R/W status. Note: Before you continue, make sure you know why B disk had R/O status – was it an accident or intentional?

USING LINE NUMBERS AND UPPER CASE TRANSLATION

15. Let's assume that you have successfully opened a new file under ED and you have this display:

```
A>ED MAILIST.DOC

NEW FILE
      : *_
```

Before you go any further, you should decide whether you want to use line numbering or not. Remember that the line numbers don't get stored in the file. ED displays them to help you move around in the file while you're editing it.

Even though we don't need them when we're typing a new file, we tend to leave them on – except when we want eight more characters on each display line. For example, our video terminal has 80 columns per line. If we use line numbering we only have 72 columns left. If we're entering 80-character records, we'll turn line numbering off so that we can get a whole record on one line.

If you want to leave line numbering on, don't do anything. If you want to turn it off, type –V and enter. The system will respond like this:

```
      : *-V
*_
```

In CP/M version 1.4, line numbering is initialized to off and you must turn it on if you want it. Type V and enter. The response looks like this:

```
*V
      : *_
```

(CP/M versions before 1.4 don't have line numbering.)

Suppose you have this display.

```
A>ED MAILIST.DOC
      : *_
```

(a) Is line numbering on or off? ______________________

(b) Show the command to change it. * ______________________

Suppose you have this display.

```
A>ED MAILIST.DOC
*_
```

(c) Is line numbering on or off? ______________________

(d) Show the command to change it. * ______________________

– – – – – – – – – – – – – – –

(a) on; (b) *–V; (c) off; (d) *V

---

16. You may also want to turn on upper case translation. The command is *U.

Suppose you have this display:

```
A>ED MAILIST.DOC
     : *_
```

Show the command to turn upper case translation on. *____________________

– – – – – – – – – – – – – – – –

*U

INSERT LEVEL

17. Now that you've decided about line numbering and upper case translation, you're ready to begin entering data. As far as ED is concerned, you're going to *insert* data into the file.

The ED command for insert is I. If you follow I immediately with <CR>, you'll enter ED's insert level. At insert level, ED will *store all characters* that you type until it encounters the terminator character, ^Z.

Up until now, all the CP/M commands you've learned have been terminated by <CR>. This is not true with the I command. If you type <CR> when inserting data, ED stores and displays <CR><LF>. But you are still in insert level. To end the insert level you must type ^Z.

(a) Show the ED command to initiate the insert level. * ____________________

(b) How do you terminate insert level and get back to ED command level?

____

(c) In insert level, what effect does <CR> have? ____________________

____

– – – – – – – – – – – – – – – –

(a) *I; (b) type ^Z; (c) inserts <CR><LF> in the data (and ends the line)

18. Now let's walk through an example of inserting data. We'll start at the CP/M command level.

with automatic line numbering	without automatic line numbering
`A>ED INDEX.DOC`	`A>ED INDEX.DOC`
`NEW FILE`	`NEW FILE`
`     : *_`	`*_`

You're now at the ED command level and ready to enter insert mode.

```
  : *I                                *I
1:  _                                 _
```

With line numbering on, you can see that ED is ready to receive line 1. With line numbering off, the lack of any prompt tells you that you're at the insert level and ED is ready to receive data.

Suppose you have this display:

```
A>ED MAILIST.DOC
NEW FILE
     : *-V
*I
_
```

(a) What level are you now at? ____________________

(b) Can you begin typing data from MAILIST.DOC? ____________________

In the display below, show what ED's response will be.

```
A>ED MAILIST.DOC
NEW FILE
     : *I
```

(c) ____________________

(a) ED insert level; (b) yes; (c) 1: _

19. Once in insert mode, all you do is type the data you want stored on the disk. What happens when you reach the end of a line and hit RETURN? ED stores a carriage return <CR> and line feed <LF> in memory and displays them on your terminal. Therefore you start a new line in your file.

With line numbering on, it looks like this:

```
1: THE THORSON COMPANY<CR>
2: _
```

Without line numbering, it looks like this:

```
THE THORSON COMPANY<CR>
_
```

In both cases, main memory now looks like this:

```
THE THORSON COMPANY<CR><LF>
```

Suppose you have this interaction:

```
A>ED MAILIST.DOC<CR>
    : *I<CR>
   1:   JUDI N. FERNANDEZ<CR>
   2:   _
```

(a) What level are you now at? ________________

(b) Can you enter an ED command? ________________

(c) Can you continue entering data in MAILIST.DOC? ________________

\- - - - - - - - - - - - - - - -

(a) ED insert level; (b) no – that is, you can type the command but ED will treat it as data for MAILIST.DOC; (c) yes

```
A>ED MAILIST.DOC<CR>
NEW FILE
     : *I<CR>
    1:   THE THORSON COMPANY<CR>
    2:   16 MAPLE ST.<CR>
    3:   SAN DIEGO, CA 92117<CR>
    4:   <CR>
    5:   DUOTECH, INC.<CR>
    6:   4590 CLAIREMONT DR.<CR>
    7:   SAN DIEGO, CA 92117<CR>
    8:   ^Z
    8: *_
```

Figure 7.1
Display to Create MAILIST.DOC

20. You just keep on typing lines until you've finished your file. Figure 7.1 shows the display for creating MAILIST.DOC.

If you make any typing errors, don't forget about the CP/M control characters. You can use them to correct the errors. Under all versions you can eliminate characters using the delete/rubout key. Remember that the deleted character is displayed and can be confusing. Use ^R to find out what the line really looks like. In later versions use ^H to backspace one character. It provides a more readable display.

In all versions, ^U, and ^X will delete the line you're on. (In the newer versions, ^X does this by backspacing which is slower than ^U.)

So far we have not figured out a way to backspace without erasing characters as we go. For example, if you want to correct the error in this line:

NOW I9 THE TIME_

you'll have to backspace:

NOW I_

and retype the remainder of the line:

NOW IS THE TIME

Another way to correct the line would be to store it as is, then correct it from ED command level later on. You'll learn the details of using D and K in the next chapter.

(a) Suppose you have this interaction:

```
1: THE THORSON COMPANY<CR>
2: 16 MAPLR_
```

How can you change the "R" to "E"? ______________________________

____

(b) If you use delete/rubout to correct an error, how can you see the corrected line?

____

(c) What are two ways to delete the line you're working on?

____

- - - - - - - - - - - - - - - -

(a) use either ^H to backspace or delete/rubout to delete the "R" then type the "E"; (b) type ^R; (c) ^X or ^U

When line numbering is on, ^R can sometimes get you into a strange situation. If you use ^R at the beginning of a line your display will look like this:

```
     5: ^R
_
```

The cursor is displayed in the line number area. You can type data but ^H will not work correctly.

If you accidentally get yourself in this situation, the best thing to do is to type one character then use ^R again. Your line number will then be restored:

```
     5: ^R
N ^R
     5: N_
```

TABBING

21. When you are inserting data, you may want to use the CP/M tab character ^I. This character causes a tab to be inserted in your stored data and immediately displayed.

On the operator's console CP/M puts tab stops in columns 1, 9, 17, 25, etc. Every time you type ^I, the cursor will jump to the next tab stop. If your echo printer is on, the same tab stops are used on the printer.

There is no way to change the tab stops without patching the CP/M program. Even if your terminal allows you to set tabs, CP/M will ignore the hardware settings when ^I is used.

(a) What columns are tab stops under ED? ____________________

(b) How do you tab to the next stop? ____________________

(c) Can you set your own tab stops? ____________________

- - - - - - - - - - - - - - - -

(a) 1, 9, 17, 25, ...; (b) type ^I; (c) not unless you patch the CP/M program

^I is a CP/M control character. It will work at any level of CP/M. We haven't discussed it before because you usually only use tabbing with ED.

22. ^H, ^U, and ^X can all be used to get back to the beginning of a line. ^U and ^X do it automatically; ^H lets you do it one character at a time. But none of these characters allow you to back up to the *previous* line. To do this you must use delete/rubout. This will eliminate the line feed and the carriage return.

As a reminder, when you type <CR>, ED automatically stores and displays *two* characters – <CR> and <LF>. If you want to eliminate the line ending you must delete both characters by pushing rubout/delete *twice.*

Also remember that CP/M displays deleted characters. You'll get a rather strange display. Before you push delete/rubout your display might look like this:

```
5: NOW IS THE TIME
6: _
```

One delete character will make your display look like this:

```
5: NOW IS THE TIME
6:
   _
```

What you see is the displayed <LF>. A second delete/rubout will make your display look like this:

```
5: NOW IS THE TIME
6:

_
```

Now you see the displayed <CR>. ^R will show you the actual condition of memory:

```
5: NOW IS THE TIME_
```

Suppose you have this display:

```
1: THE THORSONXCOMPANY
2: 16 MAPLE_
```

Notice the typo in line 1.

How can you get back to correct the typo? ______________________________

____

____

____

- - - - - - - - - - - - - - - -

Use ^X or ^U to get back to the beginning of line 2; then delete the <LF> and <CR>. Use ^H or delete/rubout to get back to the typo. ^R will help your display keep up with memory.

23. Suppose you want to store lines that are longer than the line on your console. For example, our console has 80-character lines but sometimes we want to type data records containing 100 or more characters.

You can store any line length you want. Don't type <CR> until you're ready to end the line. This might make your display look funny. Some video terminals will automatically move to the beginning of a new display line when you type too many characters, but others won't. (Our terminal has a button labeled NEW LINE ENABLE. When it's down, we get new lines automatically. When it's up, we don't.)

Why would you want a long line length? If you're working with both a line printer and a video terminal, your printer may have a longer line, Also, if you're preparing input data records for a computer program, the program dictates the length of the record.

Can you store lines in memory that are longer than your console line? ________

If so, explain how. ______________________________________

____

- - - - - - - - - - - - - - - -

Yes, just keep typing and finish the line before you type <CR>.

24. Now you've seen how to get into insert level and how to type the data you want. When your file has been typed, use ^Z to terminate the insert. You'll be returned to ED command level. For an example of a complete session, refer to figure 7.1 again.

Show the commands you would use to build a new file in memory named PRACTIC.DAT which would contain this data: THIS IS A PRACTICE FILE. Use line numbering.

(a) A> ____________________
NEW FILE

(b) : * ____________________

(c) 1: ____________________

1: *_

- - - - - - - - - - - - - - - -

(a) ED PRACTICE.DAT; (b) I; (c) THIS IS A PRACTICE FILE.^Z

25. When you terminate insert level, your data is stored in memory but is not on the disk yet. You must tell ED to write it on the disk. There are several different commands you could use.

E – Writes the data on the disk and terminates ED. You go back to CP/M command level. This is the *normal* exit.

H – Writes the data on the disk, but restarts ED for the same file. You can now change the file you've just created.

W – Writes the first line from memory to the $$$ file. The line is eliminated from memory and the other lines are moved up. W may be preceded by a number indicating how many lines should be moved. Thus, 25W means write 25 lines. A pound sign can be used to mean 65535, which usually means "all". Thus, #W means write all lines.

The H command can be used when you have finished creating a file and you want to go back and edit it. H is often used to make a backup copy in case of a power failure. The W command is used to empty memory and keep going. You'll need to do this if your file is larger than the space available in your TPA. However, H immediately writes the data on disk, whereas W may simply move it to another part of memory.

(a) Suppose you've just finished typing a new file and you want to save it on disk and terminate ED. What command would you enter?

* ____________________

(b) What response would you expect from the above command?

______ *_

______ A>_

(c) Suppose you've just finished typing a new file but it contains a lot of mistakes. You want to save it on disk and then correct it using ED commands. What command would you enter? *______

(d) What response would you expect from the above command?

______ *_

______ A>_

(e) Suppose you're at insert level and have the display shown below. Fill in the commands to empty the memory buffer and then continue inserting more lines. (Hint: You'll need several commands to do this.)

```
24: GOODTIME POOL SUPPLY
25: 118 B ST.
26: TUCSON, AZ 85730_
```

______

______

(f) Suppose you've been working about half an hour typing new lines. You're concerned that a power failure might cause a loss of all the data in memory. You want to save your current work on disk, then keep on editing. (This is standard practice at many places – it's done every half-hour or so.) Which command is better *H or *#W? ______

Why? ______

______

______

- - - - - - - - - - - - - - - -

(a) *E; (b) A>_; (c) *H or *#W; (d) *_; (e) you need to get to ED command level, save the file, then reenter insert level – ^Z followed by *#W or *26W, followed by *I; (f) *H is better because it will actually write the data on disk. *#W may only move it to another part of memory where it could also be lost.

26. Sometimes you decide to cancel the work that you've done without saving it on disk. ED allows you to do this also.

^C – The system reboot will work from the ED command level.

Q – This ED command works similarly to ^C, but asks you this question first:

Q – (Y/N)?_

If you really mean to quit, type Y. If you entered Q by mistake, type N.

O – This ED command means to return to the original file. The editing work you've done is eliminated from memory but you stay in ED and can start over.

The major difference between ˆC and Q is what happens to your files. If you use ˆC, ED has no chance to close out the files. They both remain in the disk directory. However, neither one contains data, even if you've used the W command. With Q, ED takes the time to close the files properly. The $$$ file is eliminated and the "filename" file contains lines written by W. (This is different from the situation if you were editing an existing file. You'll learn about that later.)

(a) Suppose you have this display:

```
A>ED MAILIST.DOC
NEW FILE
     : *Q
Q - (Y/N)?_
```

If you really mean to quit, what should you do? ______________________

(b) Following the above interaction, suppose you get a directory of the A disk. What files would be included in the directory?

______ MAILIST.DOC

______ MAILIST.$$$

______ neither of these

(c) Suppose you have this interaction:

```
A>ED MAILIST.DOC
NEW FILE
     : *^C

A>DIR
```

What files would be included in the directory?

______ MAILIST.DOC

______ MAILIST.$$$

______ neither of these

(d) Suppose you have the display shown below. You then realize that you're entering the wrong data. You want to eliminate the two lines and start over. Show the commands you'll need.

```
A>ED MAILIST.DOC
NEW FILE
     : *I
    1:  ANDREW W. JORDAN
    2:  25 AMES ROAD_
```

- - - - - - - - - - - - - - - -

(a) type Y; (b) MAILIST.DOC; (c) MAILIST.DOC and MAILIST.$$$; (d) ^Z followed by *O followed by *I

27. You may be wondering whether the CP/M control characters work with ED. At the ED command level, indicated by the * prompt, all the control characters work. At the insert level, indicated by no prompt, only some of the control characters work:

Work	*Don't work*
^H	^P
^I	^C
^X	^S
^U	
^R	
delete/rubout	
^Z	

If you want echo printing on while you're in insert mode, use it at ED command level before you enter the I command. You'll have to go back to ED command level to turn it off again.

At insert level, you may notice a slight difference in ^U and ^R – the pound sign is not displayed at the end of the abandoned line.

Which of the following CP/M control characters don't work at the ED insert level?

_____ (a) ^P _____ (f) ^H

_____ (b) ^R _____ (g) ^X

_____ (c) ^I _____ (h) ^U

_____ (d) ^C _____ (i) ^S

_____ (e) ^Z

- - - - - - - - - - - - - - - -

(a), (d), and (i)

ED ERROR MESSAGES

28. You've already seen some of the error messages you can get when you try to open a new file. Now we'll show you some other error messages.

If you enter an invalid ED command, you'll get a message in this format:

BREAK "s" AT x

The "s" is a symbol indicating the type of error. The x is the character ED "broke" on. We usually get this message when we forget to enter insert level and type data on command level. The interaction goes something like this:

```
A>ED EXAMPLE.DOC
NEW FILE
     : *WHO ARE YOU?
BREAK  "?" AT H
     : *I
    1:   WHO ARE YOU?
```

If you enter more data than the TPA can hold, you'll get this message: BREAK ">" AT x. Use the W command to move lines from memory to the disk. Then you can put more data in memory.

If you finish your file in memory and it's too long to fit on the disk, you'll get this message:

```
DISK OR DIRECTORY FULL

A>_
```

This is disastrous because you've been kicked out of ED without saving your data. This error must be prevented by checking the disk space with STAT *before* you initiate ED. Estimate the size of your new file. Then make sure the disk has at least that amount of space available.

(a) Suppose you have this interaction:

```
     250: THE COST OF THE PROJECT WILL BE $25,000.<CR>
BREAK ">"  AT C
        : *_
```

What's wrong? ______________________________

How can you get out of this error condition? ______________________________

____

(b) Suppose you have this interaction:

```
        : *MEMO TO ALL STAFF
BREAK "?" AT E
        : *
```

What's wrong? ______________________________

How can you get out of this error condition? ______________________________

____

(c) Suppose you have this interaction:

```
1000:         THE END^Z
1000: *E

DISK OR DIRECTORY FULL

A>
```

What's wrong? ____________________

How can you get out of this error condition? ____________________

____

How can you prevent it? ____________________

____

____

- - - - - - - - - - - - - - - -

(a) memory is full; use #W to empty memory; (b) unrecognizable ED command; use I to enter insert mode; (c) the new file didn't fit on the disk; you can't remedy this situation, you've lost the file. Always use STAT to check available space before starting a new file.

29. Summary.

In this chapter you have seen how to initiate ED, select line numbering and upper case translation, enter insert level, insert data while making corrections as necessary, save the data on disk, and terminate the edit session.

The format of command to initiate ED is:

d>ED specific-filename

The ED command prompt is a single asterisk (*), which may be preceded by a line number indicating the current position of the character pointer.

The ED commands that you have learned are:

U – turns upper case translation on
–U – turns upper case translation off
V – turns line numbers on
–V – turns line numbers off
I – initiates insert level
E – ends ED and saves file
H – saves file and restarts ED for the same file
nW – writes n lines from memory to $$$ file; # is used for 65535
Q – quits ED with no editing saved
O – returns to original file

At the ED command level, all the CP/M control characters work as usual. At the ED insert level, these control characters work:

^I – tab
^H – backspace *
^R – reshow line
^X – backspace to beginning of line
^U – delete line
delete/rubout – delete and display preceding characters
^Z – terminate insert

(*This command only works with newer versions.)

You'll practice using these commands in the Self-Test and Suggested Machine Exercises.

CHAPTER 7 SELF-TEST

1. Show the CP/M command to initiate ED for a new file named CHAPTER7.ST

   A> ______________________________

2. Match the following responses with their meaning.

   ______ a. `** FILE IS READ/ONLY **`
   `: *_`

   ______ b. `NEW FILE`
   `: *_`

   ______ c. `: *_`

   ______ d. `BDOS ERROR ON A: R/O`

   ______ e. `"SYSTEM" FILE NOT ACCESSIBLE`
   `A>_`

   ______ f. `ED?`
   `A>_`

   1. The file already exists.
   2. ED is ready to create a new file.
   3. ED.COM file is not available.
   4. The disk has read/only status and you can't put a new file on it.

3. Show the command to turn line numbering on. * ______________

4. Show the command to turn line numbering off. * ______________

5. Show the command to turn upper case translation on. * ______________

6. Show the command to turn upper case translation off. * ______________

7. Show the command to initiate insert level. *________________

8. Show the command to terminate insert level. *________________

9. On your display screen, how can you tell the difference between insert level and ED command level? ________________

____

10. What's the control character for tabbing? ________________

11. Which of these control characters work at the insert level and which work at the command level? Label I (insert), C (command), or B (both).

_____ a. ^P

_____ b. ^I

_____ c. ^S

_____ d. rubout/delete

_____ e. ^H

_____ f. ^U

_____ g. ^X

_____ h. ^C

12. Show the command to terminate ED and save the data on disk. *________

13. Show the command that will terminate ED but not save the data on disk. *____

14. Show the command to save all lines in the $$$ file and keep going. *________

15. Show the command to save the data on disk and restart ED for the same file.

*________________

16. Show the command to return to the original file and start over. *________

17. Which of the following errors is unrecoverable?

_____ a. BREAK "#" AT T

_____ b. DISK OR DIRECTORY FULL

_____ c. BREAK ">" AT D

18. How can the above error be prevented? ________________

____

____

19. What types of files can ED create?

_______ a. COM

_______ b. HEX

_______ c. other

Chapter 7 Answer Key

1. A>ED CHAPTER7.ST

2. a. 1
   b. 2
   c. 1
   d. 4
   e. 1
   f. 3

3. *V

4. *–V

5. *U

6. *–U

7. *I

8. ^Z

9. ED command level is indicated by the command prompt, *. Insert level has no prompt.

10. ^I

11. a. C
    b. B
    c. C
    d. B
    e. B
    f. B
    g. B
    h. C

12. *E

13. *Q

14. *#W

15. *H

16. *O

17. b

18. Check available disk space with STAT before initiating ED.

19. c

Suggested Machine Exercises

In this exercise you'll practice creating several short files.

In steps 1–13 you'll create a short file containing this message:

THIS IS A PRACTICE FILE.
I AM EXPERIMENTING WITH ED.

1. Start up the system. Boot from a disk that contains STAT.COM and ED.COM.
2. Use STAT to check the available space on your disk. You'll need at least 2K.
3. Repeat steps 1–3 until you have a disk with enough space.
4. Initiate ED for the PRACTICE.1 file.
5. Turn on echo printing.
6. If line numbering is off, turn it on.

7. Initiate insert level.

8. Type the file. Correct typing errors as you go.

9. Terminate insert level.

10. Save the file and terminate ED.

11. Check your disk directory. You should see PRACTICE.1 there.

12. TYPE PRACTICE.1.

    In steps 14–19 you create another practice file, without using line numbers.

13. Initiate ED for the PRACTICE.2 file.

14. Create PRACTICE.2 without using line numbering. Use the same text as PRACTICE.1.

15. Terminate ED but don't save the file. Use Q, not ^C.

16. Check your directory. PRACTICE.1 and PRACTICE.2 should both be there.

17. Type PRACTICE.2. It should be empty.

18. Erase PRACTICE.2.

    In steps 19–33, practice using the various ED features you studied in this chapter.

19. Initiate ED for PRACTICE.3.

20. Type any nonsense on the ED command line and enter it. You should get a break message.

21. Before continuing make sure echo printing is on, if you have that facility. Also turn line numbering on.

22. Initiate insert level.

23. Type a line that is longer than your console line. Compare the results on your console and your echo printer.

24. Type a few lines using tabbing to create columns. You could use this data:

JAN	FEB	MAR
APR	MAY	JUN
JUL	AUG	SEP
OCT	NOV	DEC

25. Use ^U to erase your current line.

26. Use rubout/delete to erase <LF> and <CR>. Use ^R to clear your display.

27. Use ^X to erase the line. Is there a difference between ^X and ^U?

28. You are now at the beginning of a new line. Try ^R and see what happens.

29. Does your display look like this?

    N:

    _

    If so, do you remember how to get out of this situation? Type any character, then use ^R again.

30. Terminate insert level.

31. Abort ED using ^C.

32. Check your directory. You should see PRACTICE.3 and PRACTICE.$$$.

33. Erase PRACTICE.3 and PRACTICE.$$$.

This completes our suggested machine exercise. You may want to spend more time creating some new files and experimenting with ED. When you're ready, shut down your system and go on to Chapter 8. Save the PRACTICE.1 file. You'll be using it again later.

CHAPTER EIGHT

Editing Existing Files

In this chapter we'll show you how to edit an existing file with ED. You'll learn many new commands.

When you complete this chapter, you will be able to:

- initiate ED to edit an existing file,
- move lines from the disk file to memory,
- display lines on the console,
- move the character pointer,
- delete data from memory,
- insert data in memory,
- search for and replace data in memory,
- save the edited data,
- eliminate the edited data,
- terminate ED.

1. To edit an existing file, you'll need these things available on disk:

   - ED.COM file
     - correct user number
   - the file to be edited
     - DIR status
     - same user number
     - R/W status
   - space for ED's $$$ file (at least as much space as the existing file)

To initiate the edit, enter ED specific-filename. CP/M will load ED and give it control. ED will then search the indicated disk directory for specific-filename. It also opens the $$$ file.

If specific-filename is found in the directory, ED returns the ED command prompt.

(a) Write the command to edit the file named MAILIST.DOC

A> ______________________________

(b) Suppose ED.COM is on A disk and MAILIST.DOC is on B disk. Write the command to edit MAILIST.DOC.

A> ______________________________

(c) Suppose you have logged on as user 0, ED.COM is filed under user 0, and MAILIST.DOC is filed under user 3. Can you edit MAILIST.DOC?

____

(d) Suppose ED.COM has system and R/O status and MAILIST.DOC has DIR and R/W status. Can you edit MAILIST.DOC? ______________

(e) Suppose STAT MAILIST.DOC shows that it contains 7K bytes and there are 5K bytes remaining on the disk. Can you edit MAILIST.DOC? ______________

– – – – – – – – – – – – – – – –

(a) A>ED MAILIST.DOC; (b) A>ED B:MAILIST.DOC; (c) no – the file to be edited must be filed under the same user number; (d) yes; (e) no – there's not enough room for the $$$ file

2. If all goes well, the opening dialogue should look like this (we'll assume that line numbering is on):

```
A>ED MAILIST.DOC
     : *_
```

The file has been found and ED is ready to receive commands.

But suppose ED doesn't find MAILIST.DOC for your user number. The dialogue will look like this:

```
A>ED MAILIST.DOC
NEW FILE
     : *_
```

NEW FILE is a warning message that ED didn't find the file. If you really think that MAILIST.DOC is on the disk, you'll need to get out of ED and resolve the problem. Use Q to quit ED. You'll then need to ERA MAILIST.DOC to get rid of the empty file that ED opened. Then you can use DIR and STAT to find the problem. Was the name misspelled? Is it filed under another user number? Is it on a different disk?

Suppose you want to edit the file named INDEX.DAT. Match the dialogues with their meaning.

_____ (a)
```
A>ED INDEX.DAT
NEW FILE
     : *_
```

_____ (b)
```
A>ED INDEX.DAT
     : *_
```

1. ED found the file.
2. ED didn't find the file.
3. ED found the file but it has R/O or system status.

In the dialogue below, fill in the commands you would use to get out of ED and erase undesired files.

```
A>ED INVENTY.DAT
NEW FILE
```
(c) `     : *__________`

(d) `Q - (Y/N)? ______`

(e) A> ____

(a) 2; (b) 1; (c) Q; (d) Y; (e) A>ERA INVENTY.DAT

3. If your edit file has system status you'll get this message:

```
A>ED MAILIST.DOC
"SYSTEM" FILE NOT ACCESSIBLE

A>_
```

If you really want to edit the file, change its status to DIR and try again.

If your edit file has R/O status you'll get this message:

```
A>ED MAILIST.DOC
** FILE IS READ/ONLY **
     : *_
```

The warning message tells you that you can't make any file changes. However, you can read it under ED if you want. If you really want to change the file, use Q to get out of ED, change the status to R/W, then initiate the edit again.

For the following questions assume that you want to make changes to the existing file named INVENTY.DAT.

(a) Suppose you have this dialogue:

```
A>ED INVENTY.DAT
"SYSTEM" FILE NOT ACCESSIBLE

A>_
```

What's wrong?____

____

What command would you enter? *______________________________

(b) Suppose you have this dialogue:

```
A>ED INVENTY.DAT
** FILE IS READ/ONLY **
    : *_
```

What's wrong?____

____

What command would you enter? *______________________________

- - - - - - - - - - - - - - - -

(a) the file has system status and can't be edited; A>STAT INVENTY.DAT $DIR;
(b) the file has R/O status and can't be changed; *Q (You need to quit ED so you can change the status to R/W.)

4. Let's now assume that you have successfully initiated ED and you're ready for the next step.

ED checks for the file but *does not load it.* Your data area in the TPA is empty. Before you can access, read, or change any file data, you have to load it into the TPA. You use the A command to do this. A stands for "append."

The format of the A command is: nA. The n indicates the number of lines you want ED to append. If you omit it, ED will append 1 line; that is, bring one line into the TPA.

(a) Show the command to append 5 lines. * ______________________________

(b) Show the command to append 250 lines. *______________________________

(c) Show the command to append 1 line. *______________________________

(d) Which of the following best describes the result of the A command?

_____ The indicated number of text lines are moved from memory to the disk.

_____ The indicated number of text lines are moved from the disk into memory.

_____ The indicated number of lines are displayed on the console.

- - - - - - - - - - - - - - - -

(a) 5A; (b) 250A; (c) A or 1A; (d) the indicated number of text lines are moved from the disk into memory

5. To append all the lines from the file use the command #A. In ED commands # always means 65535. With a long file, this may cause some problems. If ED can't fit the entire file into memory, you'll get this message:

```
          : *#A
BREAK ">" AT A
          : *_
```

In this situation, you'll need to use O to return to the original file (and empty memory), then commands like *100A and *100W to work on one part of the file at a time.

Suppose you have this dialogue:

```
A>ED INVENTY.DAT
          : *#A
BREAK ">" AT A
          : *_
```

What happened?

_____ (a) ED couldn't find INVENTY.DAT.

_____ (b) INVENTY.DAT is an empty file.

_____ (c) ED appended as much of INVENTY.DAT as would fit in memory.

_____ (d) INVENTY.DAT wouldn't fit in memory, so ED didn't append anything.

_____ (e) ED couldn't understand the command.

_____ (f) ED successfully appended INVENTY.DAT.

- - - - - - - - - - - - - - - -

(c)

6. A special command is 0A (zero-A). This causes ED to append lines until the memory area is about half-full (or until all lines have been appended, if that happens first).

What do you suppose the command 0W causes ED to do?

_____ (a) Write lines until the memory area is about half empty.

_____ (b) Write no lines, but empty the memory buffer.

_____ (c) Write all lines, but don't erase from memory.

- - - - - - - - - - - - - - - -

(a)

ED LINE MANAGEMENT

Before we go any further, it's necessary for you to learn how ED manages the various data areas it processes. In the frames that follow we'll show you how ED manages the source file, the temporary file, and the data area in the TPA.

7. When you enter ED MAILIST.DOC, ED searches the indicated disk directory for MAILIST.DOC. If found, it becomes the *source file.* ED establishes a *source pointer* for the file. The source pointer keeps track of how many lines have been appended from the file.

When you append lines they're copied from the source file, but they're not erased. The source file remains intact throughout the ED function. ED simply moves the source pointer so that it always points to the first "unappended" line.

Suppose MAILIST.DOC contains 100 lines.

(a) If you enter the command *10A, what lines are appended? _____

(b) If you then enter *20A, what lines are appended? _____

(c) If you then enter *#A, what lines are appended? _____

- - - - - - - - - - - - - - - -

(a) lines 1-10; (b) lines 11-30; (c) lines 31-100

8. The diagram below shows the layout of the TPA when ED is in control. The ED program takes up a portion of the TPA. The remainder is devoted to storing data lines. We call the data area the *memory buffer.* (In computer terms, a buffer is simply a memory area set aside for data storage.)

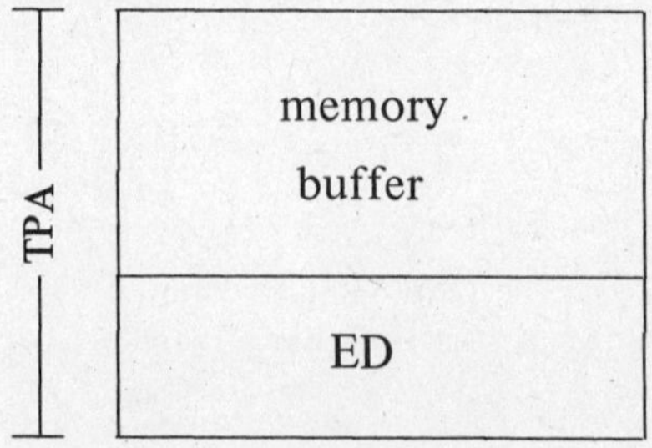

ED maintains a memory pointer that tracks the last line in memory. When you append lines, they're inserted after the memory pointer. Then the memory pointer is moved. The memory pointer keeps newly appended lines from overlaying existing lines in memory.

When you write lines using the W command, they're written from the top line through line n. Then all the remaining lines are moved up. The memory pointer is also moved. It always points to the place where the next line can be appended.

The memory pointer is not the same as the character pointer. The character pointer has a different function, as you'll learn later.

(a) Select the best definition of "memory buffer."

_____ all of main memory

_____ all of the TPA

_____ that part of the TPA that holds data lines

_____ that part of the TPA that holds ED

(b) Select the best definition of the "memory pointer."

_____ always points to the end of the memory buffer

_____ always points to the place where the next line can be appended

_____ always points to beginning of the memory buffer

- - - - - - - - - - - - - - - -

(a) that part of the TPA that holds data lines; (b) always points to the place where the next line can be appended

9. When you enter ED MAILIST.DOC, ED opens a new file called MAILIST.$$$. This is called the *temporary file.* When you write lines using the nW command, ED writes them to the $$$ file. A *temporary pointer* keeps track of how many lines are in the file so new lines don't overlay existing ones.

Suppose that the memory buffer currently contains 100 lines and MAILIST.$$$ contains no lines.

(a) If you enter *10W, which lines are erased from memory? _____

How many lines are now in MAILIST.$$$? _____

(b) If you then enter *20W, how many lines are erased from memory? _____

How many lines are in MAILIST.$$$? _____

- - - - - - - - - - - - - - - -

(a) the first 10, 10; (b) 20, 30

10. The three line pointers – source, memory, and temporary – keep you from losing, duplicating or mixing up lines. Lines are moved from the source file, to the memory buffer, to the temporary file in perfect order.

Which of the following statements is true?

______ (a) You must be careful to always follow an A command with a W command so that appended lines don't get overlaid.

______ (b) You are free to use any combination of A and W commands; ED will keep track of all lines.

______ (c) Never use more than one A command and one W command in an edit session or your lines will get mixed up.

- - - - - - - - - - - - - - - - -

(b)

Now that you've seen how ED manages all the various sets of lines, let's go back to the edit process.

DISPLAYING LINES

11. Appended lines are not automatically displayed. A typical dialogue goes like this:

```
A>ED INVENTY.DAT
     : *#A
    1: *_
```

The lines have been appended; you just can't see them. You may find this frustrating at first, but you get used to it after a while.

To display lines, use the T (type) command, which has this format: ±nT. The n gives the number of lines you want typed. The + or - indicates whether you want to go forward from the character pointer (+), or up to the character pointer (-). If omitted, + is assumed.

Suppose memory looks like this:

```
JOHN JONES<CR><LF>16 APPLE WAY<CR><LF>NEW YORK, NY 10010<CR><LF>
                          ^
```

Match the following commands with their results.

______ (a)	T	1.	JOHN JONES 16 APPLE
______ (b)	+T	2.	WAY NEW YORK, NY 10010
______ (c)	-T	3.	16 APPLE
______ (d)	2T	4.	WAY
______ (e)	-2T	5.	JOHN JONES 16 APPLE WAY NEW YORK, NY 10010
______ (f)	#T		
______ (g)	-#T		

- - - - - - - - - - - - - - - -

(a) 4; (b) 4; (c) 3; (d) 2; (e) 1; (f) 2; (g) 1

12. When lines are appended the character pointer is positioned before the first appended line. To type the lines use the nT format.

If ED couldn't append all the lines you asked for, the character pointer remains *after* the last line. To see the appended lines, you'll need to use the -nT format. Display at least -2T to get the last line.

The T command does not move the character pointer.

(a) Suppose you have this dialogue:

```
A>ED INVENTY.DAT
     : *#A
    1: *_
```

Show the command to type all the appended lines without moving the character pointer. *______________________________

(b) Suppose you have this dialogue:

```
A>ED INVENTY.DAT
     : *#A
BREAK ">" AT A
     : *_
```

Show the command to display the last appended line without moving the character pointer. *______________________________

- - - - - - - - - - - - - - - -

(a) *#T; (b) -2T

13. If you're working at a video console and you type more lines than the screen can hold, the data will roll off the top of the screen.

You can prevent this by typing one less line than your screen can hold. For example, our video console holds 24 lines so we ordinarily use the command 23T. The last line is needed for ED to return the command prompt after the T command has been processed.

If the data lines take more than one screen line each, you need to adjust the type command accordingly. Therefore if we want to type records that take two video lines each, we use the command 11T.

If we're just scanning the file we'll let it roll off the top. We use the ^S function to interrupt the display and any other character to abort the command.

Suppose you video terminal has 20 lines.

(a) What command would you use to view a screenful of lines? *________________

(b) What command would you use if the text lines each take 3 screen lines? *_____

(c) What command would you use to scan the entire file? *____________________

(d) How could you interrupt the display? *______________________________

(e) Once the display has been interrupted how can you restart the display?

*______________________________

(f) How can you abort the command? *______________________________

- - - - - - - - - - - - - - - - -

(a) 19T; (b) 6T; (c) #T or any large n such as 999T; (d) type ^S; (e) type any character except ^C; (f) type any character

14. Review.

Write the commands to edit the short MAILIST.DOC file, append all the lines, and display all the appended lines.

(a) A> ______________________________

(b) : *______________________________

(c) 1: *______________________________

(d) Where is the character pointer now?

______ at the beginning of the file

______ at the end of the file

______ somewhere in the middle of the file

- - - - - - - - - - - - - - - - -

(a) A>ED MAILIST.DOC; (b) *#A; (c) *#T; (d) at the beginning of the file

CHARACTER POINTER COMMANDS

In the following frames we'll show you the commands to move the character pointer.

15. To move the pointer a specific number of characters, use the C (characters) command which has this format: ±nC.

(a) Write the command to move the character pointer forward five characters.

*____________________

(b) Write the command to move the character pointer backward 10 characters.

*____________________

(c) Write the command to move the character pointer forward one character.

*____________________

(d) Write the command to move the character pointer backward one character.

*____________________

(e) Write the command to move the character pointer forward 65535 characters.

*____________________

(f) Write the command to move the character pointer backward 65335 characters.

*____________________

- - - - - - - - - - - - - - - -

(a) *5C or *+5C; (b) *-10C; (c) *C or *+C or *1C or *+1C; (d) *-C or *-1C; (e) *#C or *+#C; (f) *-#C

16. To move the character pointer a specific number of lines, use the L (lines) command which has this format: ±nL.

If the character pointer is in the middle of a line, it is first moved to the beginning of the line, then moved the indicated number of lines. After an L command the character pointer is always positioned at the beginning of a line. *L or *+L means *+1L; the character pointer is moved to the beginning of the current line, if necessary, then moved forward one line. *-L means *-1L; the character pointer is moved to the beginning of the current line, if necessary, then moved back one line. A special command, *0L (zero-L), moves the character pointer to the beginning of the current line.

Suppose memory looks like this:

```
ABC<CR><LF>DEF<CR><LF>GHI
             ^
```

Match the following commands with their results.

______ (a) L

______ (b) +L

______ (c) -L

______ (d) +2L

______ (e) -2L

______ (f) 0L

```
1.  ABC<CR><LF>DEF<CR><LF>GHI
   ^
2.  ABC<CR><LF>DEF<CR><LF>GHI
               ^
3.  ABC<CR><LF>DEF<CR><LF>GHI
                  ^
4.  ABC<CR><LF>DEF<CR><LF>GHI
                          ^
5.  ABC<CR><LF>DEF<CR><LF>GHI
                             ^
```

(a) 4; (b) 4; (c) 1; (d) 5; (e) 1; (f) 2

17. To move the character pointer to the beginning or end of the data lines, use the B (beginning or bottom) command, which has this format: ±B. B or +B refers to the beginning of the file, and -B refers to the end.

Match the B commands with their equivalent C and L commands.

______ (a) B

______ (b) -B

1. +#C
2. #C
3. -#C
4. -C
5. +L
6. #L
7. -#L

(a) 3, 7; (b) 1, 2, 6

18. If line numbering is on you can also move the character pointer to the beginning of a specified line. You do this by typing the line number followed by a colon, like this – 5:

You can put the line number in front of another ED command. For example, to type line 5 you would enter 5:T. To type 10 lines, starting with line 5, you would enter 5:10T. To type 3 lines up to line 5, you would enter: 5:-3T. Lines 2, 3, and 4 would then by typed (up to the character pointer).

(a) Show the command to move the character pointer to the beginning of line 100.

*____________________

(b) Show the command to move the character pointer to the beginning of line 40 and type that line. *____________________

(c) Show the command to move the character pointer to the beginning of line 10 and type lines 1-9. *____________________

(d) Show the command to move the character pointer to the beginning of line 1 and type all lines. *____________________

\- - - - - - - - - - - - - - - -

(a) *100: ; (b) *40:T or *40:+T or *40:1T or *40:+1T; (c) *10:-#T or *10:-9T; (d) *1:#T or *1:+#T

From now on we won't show you all the possible variations of a correct answer. We'll show you the preferred format, which is usually the shortest, as in *40:T above.

19. You can also specify that a command be executed *through* a line number. To do this, put the colon before the line number. For example, :10T means to type from the character pointer through line 10. The character pointer is not moved. Note that when you use this command format you can't also specify the number of lines. The command :10+5T makes no sense. You can, however, combine a beginning and ending line reference. The command 2::10T would move the character pointer to the beginning of line 2 and type lines 2 through 10. The character pointer would remain at the beginning of line 2.

Write the appropriate commands for the following functions:

(a) Type from the character pointer through line 100. *____________________

(b) Move the character pointer to line 100 and type through line 120. *__________

\- - - - - - - - - - - - - - - -

(a) *:100T; (b) 100::120T

20. You can use a special (and very convenient) abbreviation to move a specific number of lines and type the new current line. Simply enter ±n. For example, the command *5 means to move forward five lines and type. *-3 means to move backward three lines and type.

If you simply hit <CR>, ED will interpret it as +1 and move down 1 line and type.

Suppose memory contains these lines.

```
1: THIS IS LINE 1
2: THIS IS LINE 2
3: THIS IS LINE 3
4: THIS IS LINE 4
5: THIS IS LINE 5
```

Starting from line 1, state what line will be typed by each of the following commands.

(a) *<CR> ______________________

(b) *2 ______________________

(c) *<CR> ______________________

(d) *-3 ______________________

(e) *<CR> ______________________

- - - - - - - - - - - - - - - -

(a) 2; (b) 4; (c) 5; (d) 2; (e) 3

21. As long as the character pointer is within the stored data lines, the displayed line number shows which line contains the character pointer. It isn't necessarily at the beginning of that line, but it's somewhere in the indicated line. You should be able to tell where, by what happened previously.

(a) Suppose your display looks like this:

```
A>ED OLDFILE
     : *#A
    1: *_
```

Where is the character pointer? ______________________

(b) Continuing the above example:

```
1: *3T
1:  THIS IS LINE 1
2:  THIS IS LINE 2
3:  THIS IS LINE 3
1: *_
```

Where is the character pointer now? ______________________

(c) Continuing the above example:

```
1: *3
4:  THIS IS LINE 4
4: *_
```

Where is the character pointer now? ______________________

(d) Continuing the above example:

```
4: *-2L
2: *_
```

Where is the character pointer now? ______________________

(e) Continuing the above example:

```
     2: *5C
     2: *T
IS LINE 2
     2: *_
```

Where is the character pointer now? ______________________

- - - - - - - - - - - - - - - -

(a) beginning of line 1; (b) still at the beginning of line 1; (c) beginning of line 4; (d) beginning of line 2; (e) middle of line 2

DELETE COMMANDS

Now that you've learned how to move the character pointer and type lines, we'll show you how to delete data from memory.

22. To delete one or more characters from memory, use the D (delete) command. Its format is ±nD. It deletes n characters forward or backward from the character pointer. The character pointer is not moved.

Suppose your memory looks like this:

ABC<CR><LF>DE^F<CR><LF>GHI

Match the commands with their results.

______ (a) *#D		1. ABC<CR><LF>D^F<CR><LF>GHI
______ (b) *2D		2. ABC<CR><LF>DE^<CR><LF>GHI
______ (c) *-1D		3. ^F<CR><LF>GHI
______ (d) *D		4. ABC<CR><LF>DE^
______ (e) *-#D		5. ABC^F<CR><LF>GHI
______ (f) *-4D		6. ABC<CR><LF>DE^GHI
______ (g) *1D		7. ABC<CR><LF>DE^<LF>GHI
______ (h) *-D		

- - - - - - - - - - - - - - - -

(a) 4; (b) 7; (c) 1; (d) 2; (e) 3; (f) 5; (g) 2; (h) 1

23. You can see that the position of the character pointer is very important when you're using the delete commands. Don't forget that you can always find out where the character pointer is by using the T command. You can move it by using the C, L, or B commands, or absolute line references. It's also extremely important to remember that T *does not move* the character pointer.

Suppose your display currently looks like this:

```
 : *B
1: *3T
1:  JOHN JONES
2:  16 APPLE ST.
3:  NEW YORK, NY 10010
1: *_
```

(a) Where is the character pointer? ______________________

(b) Suppose you want to delete the characters "ST. ." Write the command, or commands, to move the character pointer to precede the S. *______________

____

____

____

(c) Write the command to display the new position of the character pointer.

*______________________________________

(d) What display would you expect from the command you wrote in (c)?__________

____

(e) Assuming that the character pointer now precedes "ST. ," write the command to delete these characters. *______________________

(f) Write the command to confirm that the characters were correctly deleted.

*______________________________________

- - - - - - - - - - - - - - - -

(a) at the beginning of the first line; (b) there are several ways to do this. You could use *21C (remembering to count <CR> and <LF>), or you could use *L followed by *9C, or *2L followed by *-5C, or you could use an absolute line reference as in 2:9C or 3:-5C; (c) either *T or *-T would do; (d) T should display ST.; -T should display 16 APPLE; (e) *3D; (f) *2:T would be the best choice as it would display all of line 2; *T would show whether there was anything between the character pointer and the end of the line; *-T would not do as it would only display up to the character pointer.

24. To delete entire lines, use the K (kill) command which has this format: ±nK. +K kills up *through* the next <CR><LF>. -K kills through the preceding <CR> <LF>, all the way to the next <CR><LF>.

The following diagram depicts the range of +K and -K.

```
                    -K              +K
ABC<CR><LF>DEF<CR><LF>GHI<CR><LF>
                      ^
```

Suppose your display looks like this:

```
1: *B
1: *8T
1:  JOHN JONES
2:  16 APPLE
3:  NEW YORK, NY 10010
4:
5:  MARY SMITH
6:  10 FIELDING CT.
7:  PITTSBURGH, PA 15213
8:
1: *_
```

Which of the following commands could be used to kill lines 5-8?

_____ (a) *-3K

_____ (b) *5:4K

_____ (c) *5::8K

_____ (d) *:8K

_____ (e) *8K

_____ (f) *4L followed by *4K

_____ (g) *-4L followed by *4K

- - - - - - - - - - - - - - - -

(b), (c), and (f) [(a) would kill nothing; (d) and (e) would kill lines 1-8; (g) would kill lines 1-4]

25. If the character pointer is in the middle of a line, K will kill from the character pointer through the end of the line. -K will kill from the beginning of the *preceding* line up to the character pointer. Refer to the diagram in frame 24 again and you'll see why.

Suppose your memory looks like this:

```
ABC<CR><LF>DE^F<CR><LF>GHI
```

Match the delete commands with their effect.

______ (a)	*K	1. ABC<CR><LF>^GHI
______ (b)	*-K	2. ABC<CR><LF>DE^GHI
______ (c)	*2K	3. ABC<CR><LF>^
______ (d)	*-2K	4. ^F<CR><LF>GHI
		5. ABC^F<CR><LF>GHI
		6. ABC<CR><LF>DE^

- - - - - - - - - - - - - - - - -

(a) 2; (b) 4; (c) 6; (d) 4

26. Line numbering under ED is dynamic. As you kill lines the remaining lines are renumbered instantaneously. You won't see the line numbers change however, unless you redisplay the text after every kill command. Therefore when you're using absolute line references in your commands, watch out that the numbers don't change.

Suppose your display currently looks like this:

```
7: *B
1: *8T
1:  JOHN JONES
2:  16 APPLE
3:  NEW YORK, NY 10010
4:
5:  MARY SMITH
6:  10 FIELDING CT.
7:  PITTSBURGH, PA 15213
8:
1: *_
```

(a) Suppose you enter these commands:

```
1: *3:K
3: *4:T
```

What line will be displayed?

______ 4: NEW YORK, NY 10010

______ 4:

______ 4: MARY SMITH

(b) Go back to the original display and write the commands to kill lines 2 and 6. Use absolute line references.

*______________________________

*______________________________

- - - - - - - - - - - - - - - - -

(a) MARY SMITH; (b) *2:K; *5:K

INSERT COMMAND

When you're editing an existing file you may want to insert new data. In the following frames we'll show you how to do that.

27. To insert data in memory, use the I command. I will insert the data immediately before the character pointer. You can either go into insert level, as you learned before, or include the insert data directly in the I command.

To enter insert level, type I<CR>. ED gets ready to receive new data but does not start a new line. The data you type next will be inserted before the character pointer, wherever it is.

Let's examine three cases.

In case number 1 we want to insert an apartment number in John Jones' address. First we confirm the first three lines. Then we <CR> to move down and confirm the second line. We then enter insert level and type "APT. #101". We follow it with <CR> because we want it to be a separate line, and then use ^Z to end insert level. Finally, we confirm our work.

```
1: *3T
1:  JOHN JONES
2:  16 APPLE RD.
3:  NEW YORK, NY 10010
1: *<CR>
2:  16 APPLE RD.
2: *I
2:  APT. #101<CR>
3:  ^Z
3:  1::4T

1:  JOHN JONES
2:  APT. #101
3:  16 APPLE RD.
4:  NEW YORK, NY 10010
1: *_
```

```
6: *T
6:  MARY SMITH
6: *5C
6: *I
6:  ANN ^Z
6: *6:T
6:  MARY ANN SMITH
6: *_
```

In the second case, we want to change MARY SMITH to read MARY ANN SMITH. First we get the character pointer to the desired position; between the space and the S. Then we enter insert level. We type ANN, a space, and ^Z. The four characters are inserted before the character pointer. The character pointer is still in the middle of the line so we have to use 6:T to see the whole line.

In our last case we want to put our zip code on a separate line. We want to insert <CR><LF> in between NY and 10010. First we position the character pointer. Then we enter insert level and insert <CR>. ED will automatically supply the <LF>. The <CR><LF> puts us at the beginning of line 5, where we end the insert. Then we go back to line 4 and type two lines to confirm our work.

```
4: *T
4:  NEW YORK, NY 10010
4: *13C
4: *I
4:  <CR>
5:  ^Z
5: *4:2T
4:  NEW YORK, NY
5:  10010
4: *_
```

(a) Suppose you have this display:

```
1: *4T
1:  THIS IS LINE 1
2:  THIS IS LINE
3:  THIS IS LINE 3
4:  THIS IS LINE 4
1: *_
```

You want to correct the second line so that it reads THIS IS LINE 2. Show the commands to do this. (You'll need to insert a space before the 2.)

(b) Suppose you have this display:

```
1: *4T
1:  MEMO TO ALL STAFF
2:  RE: LOCKUP PROCEDURES
3:
4:  IT HAS BEEN BROUGHT TO MY ATTENTION
1: *_
```

You want to insert a second line that reads FROM THE SECURITY OFFICER. Show the commands to do this.

There are many correct solutions to these two problems. We can't show them all so we'll show a suggested answer to each one.

(a)

```
1: *<CR>
2:  THIS IS LINE
2: *12C
2: *-T
2:  THIS IS LINE
2: *I
2:   2^Z
2: *2:T<CR>
2:  THIS IS LINE 2
2: *_
```

(b)

```
1: *2:I
2:  FROM THE SECURITY OFFICER<CR>
3:  ^Z
3: *1:3T
1:  MEMO TO ALL STAFF
2:  FROM THE SECURITY OFFICER
3:  RE: LOCKUP PROCEDURES
1: *_
```

28. You don't have to enter insert level to insert data. You can type the insert data immediately after the I command. There are two ways to terminate the insert. You can use ^Z or <CR>. <CR> will terminate the command *and* cause <CR><LF> to be inserted at the end of the new data. ^Z will simply terminate the command with no <CR><LF>.

We'll redo the three cases from the previous frame, this time without using insert level.

To insert the apartment line in John Jones' address, we first position the character pointer at the beginning of line 2. We then type the command IAPT. #101 and terminate it with <CR>. Notice that this puts us on line 3. Then we type four lines to confirm our work.

```
1: *3T
1:  JOHN JONES
2:  16 APPLE RD.
3:  NEW YORK, NY 10010
1: *<CR>
2:  16 APPLE RD.
2: *IAPT. #101<CR>
3: *1:4T
1:  JOHN JONES
2:  APT. #101
3:  16 APPLE RD.
4:  NEW YORK, NY 10010
1: *_
```

```
6: *T
6:  MARY SMITH
6: *5C
6: *IANN^Z
6: *6:T
6:  MARY ANN SMITH
6: *_
```

To change MARY SMITH to MARY ANN SMITH, we first position the character pointer. We then type the command IANN ^Z. Notice that we include a space in the command so that ANN doesn't run into SMITH. By terminating with ^Z, no <CR><LF> is inserted.

To make the zip code into a new line we first position the character pointer. Then we type the command I <CR>. We have to put a space in the command or ED will put us in insert level! The space will be inserted on line 4, but should not do any damage there. The <CR> terminates the command and inserts <CR><LF> before the 10010, putting the zip code on line 5. Don't forget that the remaining lines will be renumbered immediately.

```
4: *T
4:  NEW YORK, NY 10010
4: *13C
4:  I <CR>
5:  4:2T
4:  NEW YORK, NY
5:  10010
```

Answer the questions in frame 27 again. This time don't use insert level.

a. ____

b. ____

- - - - - - - - - - - - - - - -

Suggested answers:

a.
```
1: *<CR>
2:  THIS IS LINE
2: *12C
2: *-T
2:  THIS IS LINE
2: *I 2^Z
2: *2:T
2:  THIS IS LINE 2
2: *_
```

b.
```
1: *2:IFROM THE SECURITY OFFICER<CR>
2: *1:3T
1:  MEMO TO ALL STAFF
2:  FROM THE SECURITY OFFICER
3:  RE: LOCKUP PROCEDURES
1: *_
```

SEARCH AND REPLACE COMMANDS

By combining character pointer commands, delete commands, and insert commands, you can change a file in any way. But some types of changes would be quite tedious. For example, try going through a 1000 line report and changing all occurrences of 1989 to 1990. ED provides search and replace commands to make this task easier.

29. You can ask ED to search memory for a specified string of characters. The format of the command is Fstring. (F is for "find".) For example, if you want to find the word JONES you would enter FJONES or fJONES. ED will start at the character pointer and search forward until the five letters (JONES) are found. ED moves the character pointer to the position *after* the last character of the matching string. You can then enter an insert or delete command, or whatever is appropriate to your task.

The F command is a faster way of moving the character pointer. If your file contains both upper and lower case letters, you must use a lower case f, and the search string must match the found string exactly. For example, FJones will find "JONES". If you specify fJones, ED will find "Jones" but not "JONES" or "jones". If you use an upper case search command, you'll find upper case characters. If you use a lower case search command, you can specify exactly how the string appears. Numbers can be located either way.

(a) Write a command to search for the next occurrence of "ABCdef." *__________

(b) Where does the search start? ______________________________

(c) In what direction does the search go – forward, backward, or both?

____

____

(d) How does ED mark a matching string?

_____ by displaying the line

_____ by displaying the line number

_____ by putting the character pointer before the string

_____ by putting the character pointer after the string

- - - - - - - - - - - - - - - -

(a) *fABCdef; (b) at the character pointer; (c) forward; (d) by putting the character pointer after the string

30. Be very careful of the search strings you enter. You may get a match you didn't expect. For example, suppose memory looks like this:

```
^MEMO TO ALL STAFF<CR><LF>RE:  STAXNDING ORDERS<CR><LF>
```

You want to delete the typo in "STAXNDING" so you enter FSTA. What will happen?

```
MEMO TO ALL STAFF<CR><LF>RE:  STAXNDING ORDERS<CR><LF>
               ^
```

ED found the next occurrence of the string "STA." Your display would look like this:

```
1: *FSTA
1: *_
```

You won't necessarily know that ED found the wrong string unless you notice that you're on line 1. It's wise to always use T after F to find out exactly what ED found.

Suppose your display looks like this:

```
1: *5T
1:  JOHN JONES
2:  APT. #101
3:  16 APPLE RD.
4:  NEW YORK, NY
5:  10010
1: *_
```

It turns out that Mr. Jones' zip code is 10920. You want to find the zip code, delete 01, and insert 92.

(a) Which of the following search commands is better?

_____ F10

_____ F100

_____ F1001

_____ F10010

(b) Why? ______________________________

____

____

- - - - - - - - - - - - - - - -

(a) F1001 or f1001; (b) F10 would find the apartment number 101. F100 would find the zip code 100, but the character pointer would be in an awkward place to delete 01 and insert 92. F1001 would find 10010 and leave the character pointer in good position for *-2D followed by *I92. F10010 would also work, but you'd have to use *-3D followed by *I920.

31. The F command can be preceded by a number. For example, 3FJONES would find the *third* occurrence of JONES. The first two occurrences would be found and then bypassed.

(a) Write a command to find the second occurrence of the string "10". *__________

(b) Write a command to find the fourth occurrence of the string "Ashley."

*______________________________

- - - - - - - - - - - - - - - -

(a) *2F10; (b) *4fAshley

32. Now let's go back and redo the first problem from frame 27. This time use the F command to position the character pointer.

____

____

____

____

____

____

____

____

____

____

- - - - - - - - - - - - - - - -

____

Suggested answer:

```
1: *2FLINE
2: *-T
2:  THIS IS LINE
2: *I 2^Z
2: *-T
2:  THIS IS LINE 2
2: *_
```

You could use lower case f if you prefer.

33. If ED gets to the memory pointer without finding a match, you'll get this message: BREAK "#" AT F. The character pointer remains in its original position.

Suppose you have this display:

```
7: *B
1: *FMAX
1:  BREAK "#" AT F
1: *_
```

(a) What happened? ______________________________

____

(b) Where is the character pointer now? ______________________________

____

- - - - - - - - - - - - - - - -

(a) ED couldn't find "MAX"; (b) at the beginning of memory

34. If your file is larger than the memory buffer, you can search the whole file using the N command. An upper or lower case letter can be used with the same effect as with the F command. N combines F, W, and A commands in this fashion:

1. Text data in memory is searched. If a match is found, the command terminates normally as with F.
2. If a match is not found, all lines in memory are written to the temporary file. This is equivalent to a #W command.
3. Lines are then appended from the source file until memory is about half full or the source file is exhausted. This is equivalent to a 0A command.
4. Steps 1-3 are repeated until a match is found or the source file is exhausted.

Use this command wisely. Once lines to the temporary file have been written, you can't retrieve them again without ending the edit and starting over again.

Write a command to search the entire MAILIST.DOC file for ART DECO, LTD.

A>ED MAILIST.DOC

: *____________________

- - - - - - - - - - - - - - - - -

*NART DECO, LTD. or *nART DECO, LTD.

35. Sometimes you need to search for a string containing <CR><LF>, but you can't type <CR> or the command will be entered and processed. Use ^L as a substitute for <CR><LF>. When ED reads ^L it searches for <CR><LF>.

Write a command to search for NY<CR><LF>10010. *____________________

- - - - - - - - - - - - - - - - -

*FNY^L10010 or *fNY^L10010

Now that you've learned how to search for strings, we'll show you how to replace them.

36. Replacement is a combined process of deleting old characters and inserting new ones. You can do this with one ED command, the S (substitute) command. S combines searching, deleting, and inserting. The format is:

nSold-string^Znew-string

You can use upper or lower case S with the same effects as in the N or F command. If no *n* is given, ED will search for the next occurrence of old-string and replace it with new-string. The character pointer is left at the end of the new-string.

If *n* is given, ED searches for and replaces the next *n* strings. Therefore if n is 4, ED will make 4 replacements (if possible). The character pointer is positioned after the last replacement.

The number of characters in old-string and new-string do not need to be the same.

(a) Write a command to find *all* occurrences of JONES and replace with JOHNSON.

*____________________

(b) Can you use the S command to search for and replace only the *fourth* occurrence of Jones with Johnson? __________ If so, show the command.

*____________________

- - - - - - - - - - - - - - - - -

(a) *#SJONES^ZJOHNSON; (b) no – *4sJones^ZJohnson would replace the next four occurrences

37. The S command can be used to great advantage in some applications. For example, suppose you want to send a personalized letter to ten potential clients. You can set the text of the letter up so that an * indicates the receiver's name thus:

> Dear *,
>
> I enjoyed talking to you at yesterday's NSPI meeting.
> I indicated that I had a short-term investment program
> that you may be interested in. I've been reviewing the
> information you gave me, *, and I'm sure that this plan
> is perfect for you. Etc. Etc.

Write the command to replace all occurrences of * in this file with Bob.

*

- - - - - - - - - - - - - - - -

#s^ZBob

38. One final search and replace command gives you even more flexibility in changing a text. This is the J (juxtaposition) command.

J involves three strings – a search string, an insert string, and a termination string. This is how it works. ED searches memory for the search string. The insert string is inserted *after* the search string in memory. The two strings are placed next to each other, or juxtaposed. Finally, all characters following the insert are deleted up to the termination string.

Confusing? An example will help. Suppose we want to change all JONES to JOHNSON. We'll make JO the search string. The insert string is HNSON. The termination string is a space. Now watch what happens.

First, ED locates JO. MR. JONES

Then, ED inserts HNSON. MR. JOHNSONNES

Finally, ED deletes up to the next space. MR. JOHNSON

The format of the J command is nJsearch-string^Zinsert-string^Ztermination-string. As with the other search commands, an upper or lower case letter can be used. In the above JONES-to-JOHNSON example, the command would be
#JJO ZHNSON^Z^Z.

(a) Write a command to change all occurrences of "DUOTECH" to "DUOTECH, INC." *

(b) Write a command to change all occurrences of "DuoTech" to "DuoTech, Inc."

*

- - - - - - - - - - - - - - - -

(a) *#JDUOTECH^Z, INC.^Z ^Z; (b) *#jDuoTech^Z, Inc.^Z ^Z

39. You have now learned the search and replace commands.

- F finds a matching string and moves the character pointer, but takes no other action.
- N is like F but will search the entire file, not just what's in memory.
- S finds a matching string and substitutes another string for it.
- J finds a matching string, juxtaposes an insert string, and deletes characters up to a termination string.

If any string needs to include <CR><LF>, use ^L in the command. ED interprets ^L as <CR><LF>.

(a) Write a command to find the next occurrence of "PROJECT STAR."

*______________________________

(b) Write a command to move the character pointer to line 10 and find the third occurrence of the letter "X." *______________________________

(c) Write a command to replace the next 5 occurrences of "COMPUTER" with "SYSTEM." *______________________________

(d) Change the above command so the "COMPUTER" is changed only if it's a separate word. That is, change "OUR COMPUTER IS" to "OUR SYSTEM IS" but don't change "THE MICROCOMPUTER" or "COMPUTER-ASSISTED INSTRUCTION." *______________________________

(e) Write a command to go to line 3, find the phrase "COST FACTOR" and split the line between "COST" and "FACTOR". Delete the space between the two words so that one line ends with "COST<CR><LF>" and the next line starts with "FACTOR." *______________________________

(f) Now write a command to delete the <CR><LF> after "FACTOR" on line 4. (Assume that the character pointer is positioned at the beginning of line 4.)

*______________________________

(a) *FPROJECT STAR or *NPROJECT STAR; (b) *10:3FX;
(c) *5SCOMPUTER^ZSYSTEM; (d) *5S COMPUTER ^Z SYSTEM <CR> (We included the terminating <CR> to show that a space precedes it.);
(e) 3:JCOST^Z^L^ZF; (f) S^L^Z <CR> (Did you think to insert a space after ^Z? Otherwise "FACTOR" will run into the next word with no intervening space.)

TERMINATING ED

Let's assume now that you've made all the changes you want to the old file. In the frames that follow we'll review how to get out of ED and back to CP/M level.

40. Let's review the condition of the disk files and memory after you've made some editing changes.

The source file is still on the disk. You've moved lines from this file into memory and have changed them, but no changes have been made to the disk file itself; it's still intact and it still has the same name. The source pointer shows the number of lines that have already been appended from this file.

A temporary file called filename.$$$ also exists on the disk. If you have not written any lines, it is empty. But if you've used the W command the file would contain some edited lines. The N command may also have written some lines to the $$$ file. The temporary pointer shows how many lines this file currently contains.

The memory buffer contains the edited lines that have not yet been written to the $$$ file.

Suppose you've been editing INVENTY.DOC. Match the data areas with their contents.

______ (a)	INVENTY.DOC	1. edited lines
______ (b)	INVENTY.$$$	2. unchanged source lines
______ (c)	memory buffer	

– – – – – – – – – – – – – – – –

(a) 2; (b) 1; (c) 1

41. Let's assume now that you want to take a normal exit from ED. That is, you want to save the editing work that you've done. The command is E, for exit.

In response to the E command, ED does the following:

1. Writes all lines from main memory to the $$$ file. (Equivalent to #W.)
2. Transfers any unused lines from the source file to the $$$ file. (Equivalent to repeating #A followed by #W until the source file is empty.) Note that the $$$ file now contains a complete, edited file.
3. Renames the source file as filename.BAK. This file will stay on the disk so you can get back to your original version if you wish. If the disk already contained a filename.BAK, the earlier version is erased.
4. Renames the $$$ file with the original filename. If you edited MAILIST.DOC, then the source file becomes MAILIST.BAK and the "temporary" file becomes MAILIST.DOC.
5. Returns control to the CCP.

Suppose you edit a file named INVENTY.DOC. You make several changes, then terminate the edit with E.

(a) What files would you expect to see on the disk directory?

_____ INVENTY.DOC

_____ INVENTY.$$$

_____ INVENTY.BAK

_____ $$$.BAK

_____ INVENTY.2

(b) Which of the above files would contain the new version of INVENTY.DOC?

____

(c) Which of the above files would contain the old version of INVENTY.DOC?

____

(extra point questions)

Suppose you want to make some more editing changes to INVENTY.DOC. You enter ED INVENTY.DOC, make the changes, and enter E.

(d) Where is the *third* version of INVENTY.DOC? _______________

(e) Where is the *second* version of INVENTY.DOC? _______________

(f) Where is the *original* (or first) version of INVENTY.DOC? _______________

(g) Suppose you want to create and keep five versions of the INVENTY file on the same disk. After you create the second version, what should you do before you enter ED INVENTY.DOC again?

____

____

(h) You should never try to edit a BAK file. Why?

____

____

____

____

- - - - - - - - - - - - - -

(a) INVENTY.DOC and INVENTY.BAK; (b) INVENTY.DOC; (c) INVENTY.BAK; (d) on INVENTY.DOC; (e) on INVENTY.BAK; (f) erased and gone forever; (g) rename INVENTY.BAK as INVENTY.V1 or INVENTY.ORG or some other name so that it doesn't get erased; (h) when the E command is processed, ED erases any existing filename.BAK. Your original file will be erased. ED will then attempt to rename filename.BAK (the original file, which just got erased) as filename.BAK. This command will fail, because there is no file to be renamed.

42. Suppose you want to get out of ED without saving your editing changes. The command is Q. ED will do the following.

1. Confirm that you mean to quit.
2. Erase the $$$ file.
3. Leave the original file alone.
4. Return control to the CCP.

Suppose you enter ED INVENTY.DOC. You then append some lines, make some changes, write some lines, append more lines, and make more changes. Then you enter the Q command.

(a) What files would you expect to find on the disk directory?

_____ INVENTY.DOC

_____ INVENTY.BAK

_____ INVENTY.$$$

(b) Which of the above files, if any, contains your original version of INVENTY.DOC?

____

(c) Which of the above files, if any, contains the lines that you wrote while editing?

____

Suppose you used ^C to exit ED instead of the Q command.

(d) What files would you expect to find on the disk directory?

_____ INVENTY.DOC

_____ INVENTY.BAK

_____ INVENTY.$$$

(e) Which of the above files, if any, contains your original version of INVENTY.DOC?

____

(f) Which of the above files, if any, contains the lines that you wrote while editing?

____

- - - - - - - - - - - - - - - -

(a) INVENTY.DOC; (b) INVENTY.DOC; (c) none; (d) INVENTY.DOC and INVENTY.$$$; (e) INVENTY.DOC; (f) INVENTY.$$$

43. Don't forget about the H and O commands we mentioned in Chapter 7. The O (original) command eliminates your editing work and lets you start over. When you enter O, ED does the following:

1. Confirms that you want to return to the source file.
2. Erases the $$$ file.
3. Moves the source pointer to the beginning of the source file again.
4. Opens a new $$$ file.
5. Returns the ED command prompt.

The H (head) command saves your editing work and lets you start doing some more editing. When you enter H, ED does the following:

1. Finalizes the $$$ file – transfers all remaining lines from memory and from the source file.
2. Erases any existing filename.BAK.
3. Renames the source file as filename.BAK.
4. Renames the $$$ file as filename.typ.
5. Opens the newly named filename.typ file as the source file
6. Opens a new $$$ file.
7. Returns the ED command prompt.

(a) Which command is equivalent to *E followed by A>ED filename? ____________

(b) Which command is equivalent to *Q followed by A>ED filename? ____________

(c) Which command will cause you to eventually lose your original source file if you take a normal exit from ED? ____________

(d) With which command will you need to append more lines to continue editing?

____

(extra point question)

(e) Suppose you used an N command and most of your lines got written out to the $$$ file. But you want to do more editing on the lines that were written. You can't append them because the A command reads lines from the source file, not the $$$ file. What can you do?

____

- - - - - - - - - - - - - - - -

(a) H; (b) O; (c) H; (d) both; (e) use H to restart ED using the new file

Now you've seen how to edit an existing file using ED. You've learned how to initiate the edit, append lines, move the character pointer around, display lines, delete characters or lines, insert data, find data, replace data, juxtapose data, and end the edit session. The Self-Test will give you a chance to review and practice the material you've studied. You'll then get a chance to actually try your hand at changing the file you created before.

1: MEMO TO ~~ALL~~ SENIOR STAFF

2: FROM THE SECURITY OFFICER

3: RE: ^NIGHTLY LOCKUP PROCEDURES

4: DATE: 5/14/82

5: IT HAS BEEN ~~BROUGHT~~ CALLED TO MY ATTENTION THAT STAFF

6: MEMBERS HAVE NOT BEEN PROPERLY SECURING THE

7: BUILDING AT NIGHT. THE LAST PERSON TO LEAVE

8: THE BUILDING MUST FOLLOW THESE PROCEDURES:

9:

10: 1. ENSURE THAT ALL WINDOWS ARE LOCKED.

11:

12: 2. UNPLUG THE COFFEE POT.

13:

14: 3. TURN OFF ALL LIGHTS. ~~EXCEPT THE~~

15: ~~CENTRAL HALL~~.

16: 4. TURN OFF THE OUTSIDE LIGHTS

17: 5. ~~4~~. BOLT THE BACK ~~EXIT~~ DOOR FROM THE

18: INSIDE.

19:

20: 6. ~~5~~. LEAVE BY FRONT ~~EXIT~~ DOOR.

21:

22: 7. ~~6~~. USE KEY TO LOCK FRONT ~~EXIT~~ DOOR.

23:

24: ~~VIOLATIONS WILL BE PUNISHED~~.

25: E. J. LOCKWOOD

Figure 8.1. SECURITY.MEM File

CHAPTER 8 SELF-TEST

For this Self-Test, we'll go through the corrections to the file shown in figure 8.1. The typed material shows the SECURITY.MEM file as it currently exists. The handwritten material shows the desired corrections.

1. Write the command to initiate the edit. A> ____________

2. Match each response with its meaning.

______ (a)	`NEW FILE` `: *_`	1. file is ready for editing.
______ (b)	`: *_`	2. ED couldn't open a directory for the temporary file
______ (c)	`** FILE IS READ/ONLY**`	3. file was not found
______ (d)	`DISK OR DIRECTORY FULL` `A>_`	4. file has R/O status
______ (e)	`"SYSTEM" FILE NOT ACCESSIBLE` `A>`	5. file has system status

3. Assume that you got the correct response and go on to the next step. Show the command to append all the lines. *____________

4. Match each response with its meaning.

______ (a)	`1: *_`	1. no lines were appended
______ (b)	`BREAK ">" AT A` `: *`	2. some, but not all, lines were appended
		3. all lines were appended

5. Assume that all lines were appended and go on to the next step. Write one command to change ALL to SENIOR in line 1.

   *____________

6. Write one command to insert NIGHTLY in line 3.

   *____________

7. Write one command to insert the new fourth line. We still want the blank line before the start of the text of the memo.

   *____________

   Remember that all your lines have now been renumbered.

8. Write one command to change BROUGHT to CALLED.

   *____________

9. Write one command to position the character pointer after LIGHTS in the third point. *______

10. Write one command to delete EXCEPT THE CENTRAL HALL, leaving the period after LIGHTS. *______

11. Instead of questions 9 and 10, you could have used one J command to accomplish the same function. Show the command. *______

12. Write one command to insert the new step 4. Maintain the double-spacing before and after the line. *______

13. Write one command to change all the EXITs to DOOR.

*______

14. Write the commands to change 4 to 5, 5 to 6, and 6 to 7. (Hint: Step 5 is now on line 19.)

*______

*______

*______

15. Write one command to delete the line containing VIOLATIONS WILL BE PUNISHED. (Hint: It's now line 26.)

*______

16. Write one command to display the entire corrected file.

*______

17. Write the command to end the edit normally and save your work.

*______

18. Match these responses with their meanings.

______ a. A>_	1. the file has been saved
______ b. DISK OR DIRECTORY FULL	2. the source file was lost
	3. the editing work was lost
	4. the source file is still there

19. Assuming you got a normal response, what files will appear on the disk directory?

_____ a. SECURITY.MEM

_____ b. SECURITY.DAT

_____ c. SECURITY.$$$

_____ d. SECURITY.BAK

20. Which of the above files contains the original text? _____________________

21. Which of the above files contains the new text? _____________________

22. Match the following commands with their functions.

_____ a. E		1. empty memory buffer
_____ b. H		2. finalize and rename $$$ file
_____ c. O		3. rename source file as BAK file
_____ d. Q		4. erase $$$ file
_____ e. #W		5. new source file
		6. reopen old source file
		7. terminate ED
		8. continue ED

Chapter 8 Answer Key

1. `A>ED SECURITY.MEM`

2. a. 3
   b. 1
   c. 4
   d. 2
   e. 5

3. `*#A`

4. a. 3
   b. 2

5. *SALL^ZSENIOR

6. *JRE: ^ZNIGHTLY ^ZL

7. *4:IDATE: 5/14/82<CR>

8. *SBROUGHT^ZCALLED

9. *FLIGHTS

10. *D33 (Did you remember to delete the eight spaces preceding CENTRAL HALL, as well as the <CR><LF>?)

11. *JLIGHTS^Z^Z.

12. *17:I   4. TURN ON THE OUTSIDE LIGHTS.^L<CR>

13. *#SEXIT^ZDOOR

14. *19:S4^Z5
    *S5^Z6
    *S6^Z7

15. *26:K

16. *1:#T or *B#T

17. *E

18. a. 1, 4
    b. 3, 4

19. a, d (b could appear if it was present before editing.)

20. d

21. a

22. a. 1, 2, 3, 7
    b. 1, 2, 3, 5, 8
    c. 1, 4, 6, 8
    d. 4, 7
    e. 1, 8

Suggested Machine Exercises

In these exercises you'll edit the PRACTICE.1 file that you created at the end of Chapter 7. We'll leave you to decide what steps you want to follow. Be sure to practice using insert, delete, and the search and replace commands. The corrected copy is shown below.

```
THIS WAS A PRACTICE NEW FILE.
NOW IT'S A PRACTICE OLD FILE.
I AM EXPERIMENTING WITH ED'S
FILE EDITING FEATURES.
```

Save the edited file; you'll use it again at the end of Chapter 9. You can erase PRACTICE.BAK.

CHAPTER NINE

Advanced ED Functions

You've now learned the basic ED commands and should be able to handle any editing function you need. However there are more facilities available under ED that make your job faster and easier. You'll learn those features in this chapter.

When you complete this chapter, you will be able to:

- display the amount of space left in memory,
- page through a file,
- create and use combined commands,
- create and use macros,
- put ED to sleep,
- create and use libraries,
- place the revised file on a different disk.

TWO NEW COMMANDS

In this section, we'll introduce two new ED commands.

1. When you're making major editing changes, you may want to check on your available memory buffer area. The command 0V will result in this display:

free-space/total-space

For example, if your data space in the TPA is 30000 bytes and you've filled 2000 bytes with text lines, *0V would result in:

```
10000/30000
```

You've got 10,000 characters still available. You can now estimate how may more lines you can append or insert before running out of memory space.

(a) What command results in the display shown below? *________________

```
10000/12000
```

(b) If you're working with lines that average 50 characters each, approximately how many more lines can you append or insert? ________________

- - - - - - - - - - - - - - - -

(a) *0V; (b) about 200

2. The P command causes ED to display a 23 line "page" and move the character pointer to the top of that page. The page size assumes that you have a 24-line video terminal and your text lines are less than or equal to your screen line length.

The format of the command is ±nP. The command 0P displays the next 23 lines and does not move the character pointer.

The simple command, P, displays 46 lines and moves the character pointer down 23 lines. On a 24-line screen the first 23 lines roll off the top, leaving the second 23 lines visible. The character pointer is pointing to the first *visible* line.

Suppose you want to scan your file from the video console. You want to scan pages of 23 lines each with the character pointer always pointing to the top screen line. Your display looks like this:

```
A>ED INVENTY.DOC
     : *#A
   1: *_
```

(a) What command will display the first page? *________________

(b) Following the above command, what command will display the second page (lines 24–46)? *________________

(c) Following the above command, what command will display the third page (lines 47–69)? *________________

- - - - - - - - - - - - - - - -

(a) *0P or *23T; (b) *P or *24:23T; (c) *P or *47:23T

3. The command -P displays the 46 lines preceding the character pointer and moves the character pointer back 23 lines. The effect is to move back one 23-line page.

(a) Write a command to view the next page. *________________

(b) Write a command to view the preceding page. *________________

- - - - - - - - - - - - - - - -

(a) *P; (b) *-P

4. The P command is meant for scanning pages on a 24-line video console, when each data line takes less than a full screen line.

Under what conditions will P *not* have the intended effect?

______ (a) When the text lines are longer than the video screen.

______ (b) When the file contains more than 150 lines.

______ (c) When the video console doesn't have 24 lines.

______ (d) When the video console doesn't have upper case translation.

______ (e) When the console is a teletype-style terminal.

- - - - - - - - - - - - - - - - -

a, c, e

COMBINED COMMANDS

So far you have been using single ED commands. That is, you have only typed and entered one command at a time. But many ED commands can be combined so that you can accomplish several functions in one step. We'll show you how in the following frames.

5. To combine commands, simply string them together on the command line. ED will process the commands from left to right.

For example, suppose you enter this command: -10L3K. ED will move the character pointer up ten lines, then kill three lines. Note that the -10 goes with the L and the (+)3 goes with the K.

(a) Write a command line to append 100 lines, move the character pointer down to the bottom, and display the last line. *______________________

(b) Write a command to write 500 lines and display the amount of available space in memory. *______________________

- - - - - - - - - - - - - - - - -

(a) *100A-B-2T or *100A100:T; (b) *500W0V

6. The F, S, N, I, and J commands all involve character strings. They can be combined with other commands, but you need to mark the end of each character string with ^Z. If the character string is not followed by another command, it doesn't need to be marked. The final character string can be terminated by <CR>.

Here are some examples of combined commands containing character strings.

```
*3FJONES^Z-3CIA<CR>
```

This command will find the third occurrence of JONES, back up the character pointer to JO^NES, and insert an A. The final result will be JOA^NES.

```
*3FJONES^Z-3CIA^Z3C-T<CR>
```

This will do the same as the first command. In addition, this command will move the character pointer to the end of the word, then display the entire line up to that point.

(a) Write a command to find the next occurrence of COST FACTOR and display the line up through the string. *____________________

(b) Write a command to go to the beginning of memory, find the third occurrence of 1989, delete the 89, insert 90 instead, and display the corrected line.

*____________________

- - - - - - - - - - - - - - - - -

(a) `*FCOST FACTOR^Z-T<CR>`; (b) `*B3F1989^Z-2DI90^Z0LT<CR>`

7. Your commands are getting longer now and it's time to mention the CP/M limit on command length. A CP/M command can contain up to 255 characters. ED places a further limit on F, S, N, and J commands; they are limited to 100 characters.

Suppose you need to type a command that's longer than the length of your console line. You can use ^E to force your console to start a new line *without* affecting the command. In other words, <CR><LF> will be displayed but not stored as part of the command.

Suppose you want to search for this entire sentence:

NOW IS THE TIME FOR ALL GOOD MEN.

and replace it with this sentence:

THE QUICK BROWN FOX JUMPS.

Suppose also that your console only has 25 characters to a line. Use the boxes below to show how you would enter the command.

				1	:		*																	

- - - - - - - - - - - - - - - -

				1	:		*	S	N	O	W		I	S		T	H	E		T	I	M	E	^E
	F	O	R		A	L	L		G	O	O	D		M	E	N	.	^	Z	T	H	E		^E
Q	U	I	C	K		B	R	O	W	N		F	O	X		J	U	M	P	S	.			

8. Certain commands may not be combined with any others. They are: E, H, O and Q. When you want to terminate ED you must use a separate command to do it.

Which of the following commands can be used in combination?

_____ (a) Q _____ (e) K

_____ (b) I _____ (f) O

_____ (c) P _____ (g) H

_____ (d) E _____ (h) F

- - - - - - - - - - - - - - - -

(b), (c), (e), and (h)

9. Let's try some more combinations before going on.

(a) Write one command to append and display all the lines in a short file.

* ____

(b) Write one command to append all the lines and display lines 100 through 120.

* ____

(c) Do you remember this problem? 2: 16 APPLE ST. Write one command to move the character pointer to line 2, then move it in 8 characters, delete the next 3 characters, move it to the beginning of the line, and display the entire line.

* ____

(d) Do you remember this one? 5: MARY SMITH. Write one command to find MARY, insert ANN, and display the entire line.

* ____

(e) Write one command to insert a second line containing APT. #101 and display the first three lines. *____________________

(f) Write a command to append all the lines, change all EXITs to DOOR, and display the entire file. *____________________

- - - - - - - - - - - - - - - - -

(a) `*#A#T;` (b) `*#A100::120T;` (c) `*2:8C3D2:T;` (d) `*FMARY ^ZIANN ^ZOLT;`
(e) `*2:IAPT. #101^L^ZB3T;` (f) `*#A#SEXIT^ZDOOR^ZB#T`

MACROS

Sometimes we want to repeat a combined command more than once. You can write a macro and have it repeated any number of times. The following frames will show you how.

10. The format of an ED macro is: nMcombined-command. ED will repeat the combined command, from left to right, the number of times you specify.

For example, look at this macro: *5MF89^Z-2T. ED will find the next occurrence of "89" and display the two lines leading up to it. Then go on and find the *next* occurrence of "89" and display the two lines leading up to that. This will continue until the entire macro has been repeated, left to right, 5 times. This is quite different from the command *5F89^Z-2T which would find the fifth occurrence of 89 and display the two lines leading up to it. If a macro is combined with other commands, it must be the last part of the command line.

Match the commands below with their functions.

_____ (a)	*B10LK	1. Kill lines 2, 4, 6, 8,. . .20
_____ (b)	*B10MLK	2. Kill lines 11-20, 31-40, 51-60, . . . 191-200.
_____ (c)	*B10L10K	3. Kill lines 11-20.
_____ (d)	*B10M10L10K	4. Kill line 11.

- - - - - - - - - - - - - - - - -

(a) 4; (b) 1; (c) 3; (d) 2

11. In a macro every character string must be terminated by ^Z, including the final one. Write a macro that will start at the beginning of the file, find every occurrence of 1989, and change the 89 to 90. Use the extended search capability of the N command.

*____________________

- - - - - - - - - - - - - - - - -

```
*B#MN1989^Z-2DI90^Z
```

Explanation:

- B sends the character pointer to the beginning of the memory buffer.
- #M causes the macro to be repeated up to 65535 times.
- N1989 searches (extended) for the next occurrence of 1989. The character pointer is positioned after the matching string.
- ^Z marks the end of the search string.
- -2D deletes the preceding two characters which will always be "89".
- I90 inserts 90 in front of the character pointer.
- ^Z terminates the 90.

12. If you omit the number in front of M the macro is repeated until some outside circumstance stops it. Usually it repeats until it encounters a command that it can no longer execute because it has reached the end of data in memory, the end of memory, or the end of the file.

(a) When will this macro end – *M66L3T? ______________________

____

____

(b) When will this macro end – *MN1989^Z-4D? ______________________

____

____

– – – – – – – – – – – – – – – –

(a) at the end of data in the memory buffer, when ED can't move down 66 more lines; (b) when the entire source file has been exhausted and ED can't find another 1989

13. A macro always ends on a BREAK message. Even if you limit the number of times it's executed, you'll still get a BREAK message.

Suppose you have this display:

```
     1:  *3M66LT
    67:   TANDEM REPORT - PAGE 2
   133:   TANDEM REPORT - PAGE 3 (REVISED)
   199:   TANDEM REPORT - PAGE 3
BREAK   "#" AT L
   199:  *_
```

What happened?

______ (a) The macro executed successfully.

______ (b) ED encountered some error and could not finish executing the macro.

– – – – – – – – – – – – – – – –

(a) (You can see that ED typed lines 67, 133, and 199 and left the character pointer at the beginning of line 199.)

14. Did you know that you can tell ED to go to sleep? The command is nZ. The n specifies the number of seconds ED should sleep. We use the Z command to force ED to pause for a specific period of time while processing a repetitive macro. This gives us time to cancel the macro if we want to.

For example, suppose we want to search the file for all occurrences of JONES and replace them with SMITH. However but we want to take a cautious approach and view each JONES before it gets replaced. The command we might use is: *BMNJONES^Z-2T10Z-5DISMITH^Z-2T5Z<CR>. This will cause the following actions:

1. Move the character pointer to the beginning of memory.
2. Execute the macro until a BREAK occurs.
   a. Search for the next occurrence of JONES.
   b. Display the two lines preceding the found string, up through JONES.
   c. Sleep 10 seconds, giving us a chance to read the displayed lines and cancel the command if we don't want to the change to be made.
   d. Delete JONES.
   e. Insert SMITH.
   f. Display the result.
   g. Sleep another 5 seconds.
   h. Repeat the macro.

We can abort the command at any time by typing any character.

Suppose we want to search the entire file (not just memory) for the phrase COST PLUS. We're looking for a particular sentence that we want to change. We want to view each occurrence of COST PLUS for about 5 seconds. When we find the right sentence, we'll abort the command. Write the command to do this.

*______________________________

— — — — — — — — — — — — — — — —

*BMNCOST PLUS^Z-2T5Z<CR> (We recommend displaying two preceding lines in case the found string is at the beginning of a line. You'll get a better idea of the context with two lines.)

LIBRARIES

ED allows you to insert an existing file into your current file. The existing file must be of type LIB, for library. We'll show you how to use libraries in the following frames.

15. To insert a LIB file into your file use the ED command R (read). Its format is Rfilename. Do not include the filetype. It's assumed to be LIB. The library file will be inserted in front of the character pointer.

Suppose the disk contains a file named CONFID.LIB containing this text:

```
1: THIS REPORT IS COMPANY CONFIDENTIAL.
2: DO NOT REMOVE FROM THE PREMISES.
```

Now you're editing a file called ANNUAL.REP. Write the command to insert CONFID.LIB as lines 65 and 66. *________________________________

\- - - - - - - - - - - - - - - - -

*65:RCONFID (Don't forget to omit the filetype in the R command.)

16. If you want to use R in a combined command you must put ^Z after the filename or ED can't find the next command.

ED will not accept a command in the format nRfilename. You can use R in a macro. The filename must be terminated with ^Z, even if it's the last command in the macro.

(a) Write the command to move down 64 lines, insert CONFID.LIB, and display the preceding three lines. *________________________________

(b) Write a macro to start at the beginning of memory and insert CONFID.LIB as every 65th and 66th line. Limit the macro to ten iterations. (We'll explain why in a minute.)

*____

\- - - - - - - - - - - - - - - - -

(a) *64LRCONFID^Z-3T; (b) *B10M64LRCONFID^Z

17. You can also create a temporary library file while editing. The command is nX, where n indicates the number of lines to place in the file – starting at the character pointer, of course. The lines are not removed from the current file.

The temporary file, named X$$$$$$$.LIB, can then be inserted in your current file by the simple command R. The filename is omitted when you want to reference the temporary library file. When necessary, R should be terminated by ^Z so ED doesn't try to read the next characters as part of a filename.

Suppose you want to move paragraph 3, lines 15-20, to follow line 35. Write the commands to:

(a) Make lines 15-20 into a temporary LIB file. *________________________

(b) Insert the temporary LIB file after line 35. *________________________

(c) Delete lines 15-20. *____

- - - - - - - - - - - - - - - -

(a) *15:6X or *15::20X; (b) *36:R; (c) *15:6K or 15::20K

18. The R command should be used cautiously in an unlimited macro. If ED reaches the end of data, it will continue to process the R command repeatedly until something stops it. It will fill your memory buffer with repetitions of the library file until memory is full or until you interrupt the process.

Suppose you want to repeat line 1 at the top of every page. (That is, after every 66th line.)

(a) Which of the following macros would be better?

______ *BXLM65LR^Z

______ *BXLM65LR^Z3T5Z

(b) Explain your choice.

____

____

____

____

- - - - - - - - - - - - - - - -

(a) *BXLM65LR^Z3T5Z; (b) because it gives us a chance to identify when the end of the data has been reached and interrupt

19. If you issue a second X command, the lines are *appended* to the temporary LIB file. Enter the command 0X if you want to erase the temporary LIB file first.

Write a command to clear the temporary LIB file and put lines 13-18 there.

*____

- - - - - - - - - - - - - - - -

*0X13::18X is one way to write the command

20. The temporary LIB file is erased by either of the termination commands: E or Q. If you terminate by ^C the file will not be erased. You can erase it yourself or let the next edit session erase it. However if you use X again before the X$$$$$$$.LIB file is erased, remember that the lines will be added to the old file.

(a) Suppose you terminate an edit session by ^C. You used the X command during the session. What files would you expect to see on the disk directory?

______ filename.typ

______ filename.BAK

______ filename.$$$

______ filename.LIB

______ X$$$$$$$.LIB

(b) Write the command to erase the temporary LIB file.

A> ____

(c) Do H and O erase the temporary file? ____________________

- - - - - - - - - - - - - - - -

(a) filename.typ, filename.$$$, and X$$$$$$$.LIB (you could have the other files if they were present before the edit); (b) A>ERA X$$$$$$$.LIB; (c) no

SWITCHING DISKS

When you're editing an existing file you can simultaneously move it to another disk. The next few frames will show you how.

21. If you want the edited file to appear on a different disk from the source file, use this command format:

d>ED filename d:

ED will open the $$$ file on d:. As you know, this eventually becomes the edited file. The BAK file remains on the original disk.

(a) Write a command to edit INVENTY.DOC on A disk and place the edited file on B disk. A> ____

(b) Write a command to edit MAILIST.DOC from B disk and place the file on A disk. A> ____

(c) After the above edit, where will MAILIST.BAK be? ____________________

(d) Suppose you enter this command A>ED PRACTICE.1 B: and get this response: FILE EXISTS. What do you suppose the message means?

____

____

- - - - - - - - - - - - - - - -

(a) A>ED INVENTY.DOC B: ; (b) A>ED B:MAILIST.DOC A: ; (c) on B disk; (d) there's already a PRACTICE.1 on B disk

22. Summary. In this chapter you've seen how to display memory space, move and display pages, write combined commands, write macros, create and use libraries, and move edited files to other disks. The commands you've studied are:

d>ED	filename d: put edited file on d:
0V	display memory space
±nP	move and print pages
nM	macro
Rfilename	insert LIB file
R	insert temporary LIB file
nX	create temporary LIB file
0X	clear temporary LIB file

CHAPTER 9 SELF-TEST

1. Write a command to display the amount of memory space available.

   *______________________________

2. Write a command to display the next 46 lines and move the character pointer down 23 lines. *______________________________

3. Write a command to append the first 100 lines, replace all "*" with "JANET" and display all the lines. *______________________________

4. Revise your above command so that 24 lines are displayed at a time, with a 30 second pause after each display. *______________________________

5. Write a command to copy lines 1-5 100 times, starting on line 6.

   *______________________________

6. Assume that you have just initiated ED and your memory buffer is empty. Write a command to completely search the source file substituting JOHN for the * character. *______________________________

7. Write a command to copy the STARS.LIB file into your current file, beginning at line 100. *____________________

8. Write a command to copy the STARS.LIB file after every existing tenth line. (Don't count the lines that are added by the command.) Terminate the command after 10 iterations. *____________________

9. Revise the above command so that you can terminate it manually from the keyboard when it's obvious that the existing lines have been finished.

   *____________________

Chapter 9 Answer Key

1. `*OV`

2. `*P`

3. `*100A#S*^ZJANET^ZB#T`

4. `*100A#S*^ZJANET^ZBM24T30Z24L`

5. `*1::5X6:100MR^Z`

6. `*MN*^Z-DIJOHN^Z`

7. `*100:RSTARS`

8. `*10M10LRSTARS^Z`

9. `*M10LRSTARS^Z-2T2T10Z`
   (You may have chosen to display a different set of lines and to "sleep" a different number of seconds)

Suggested Machine Exercises

1. First of all, build yourself a STARS.LIB file that contains two rows of asterisks.
2. Then edit the PRACTICE.1 file. It should currently contain 4 lines. Using a temporary LIB file, copy those 4 lines 100 times.
3. Your file should now contain 400 lines. Try using the P command to view them.
4. Use 0V to check your available memory space.
5. Now insert the STARS.LIB file after every fourth line so your whole file looks like this:

```
THIS WAS A PRACTICE NEW FILE.
NOW IT'S A PRACTICE OLD FILE.
I AM EXPERIMENTING WITH ED'S
FILE EDITING FEATURES.
******************************
******************************
(repeated 100 times)
```

6. Now see if you can enter a macro that will delete one row of stars from every set.

This concludes the machine exercises for this chapter. Save the PRACTICE.1 and PRACTICE.BAK files to work with in Chapter 10. It doesn't matter what state PRACTICE.BAK is in. You can erase the STARS.LIB file or experiment with it some more if you wish. When you're ready, go on to Chapter 10.

CHAPTER TEN

Submitting Command Files

CP/M commands are generally submitted one at a time. If you want to copy several specific files from one disk to another, you generally use several successive PIP commands. The CP/M SUBMIT program allows you to submit a batch of commands at one time. Then all the commands are processed before control returns to you at the console.

In this chapter you'll learn to use the CP/M SUBMIT command, as well as the XSUB command which extends the power of SUBMIT.

When you complete this chapter, you will be able to:

- Create a command file using symbolic parameters,
- Create a command file that includes the XSUB command and line input,
- Execute the command file using SUBMIT with actual parameters.

1. The SUBMIT command is used to execute all the commands in a file of filetype SUB. A SUB file always contains a list of CP/M commands. Let's assume, for now, that the SUBMIT.COM file and the SUB file are both on disk A. You'll see later that the effect may be different on other drives.

Here is an example, stored as the file CLEAN.SUB.

```
ERA *.BAK
DIR
```

If you enter the first command, all files with filetype BAK are erased. The second command simply displays a directory. The two commands will be executed by CP/M when you enter the command SUBMIT CLEAN. Of course, SUBMIT.COM must be on the active drive. Suppose file CLEAN2.SUB contains these commands:

```
ERA *.BAK
ERA *.REL
DIR
```

(a) What one command will execute all these? ______________________

(b) How is the effect different from the above example? ______________

____

(c) Modify CLEAN2.SUB so that the size of each COM file will be displayed instead of a complete directory.

____

____

- - - - - - - - - - - - - - -

(a) SUBMIT CLEAN2; (b) all existing REL files are erased as well; (c) eliminate DIR, use STAT *.COM in its place.

2. A command file is a file with filetype SUB that is intended to be used with the SUBMIT command. The files CLEAN.SUB and CLEAN2.SUB are both command files. These are sometimes called submit files. You've seen CP/M built-in commands in a command file. Any CP/M transient commands, such as PIP or STAT, or any other command (COM file) can be included in a command file. We'll soon see how to specify parameters and line entries when a file is submitted.

Suppose you copy the same four files (PIP, STAT, ED and SYSGEN) onto every new disk you use.

(a) Write a command file that you could execute with SUBMIT MAKECPM to copy the four files onto drive B from the current drive.

____

____

____

____

(b) What is the name of the file you have written?

____

- - - - - - - - - - - - - - -

(a)
```
PIP B:=PIP.COM
PIP B:=STAT.COM
PIP B:=ED.COM
PIP B:=SYSGEN.COM
```

(b) `MAKECPM.SUB`

3. Often the information you need in a command file may vary from one submission to the next. For example, if your setup includes more than two drives, you may want to be able to specify the destination drive, as in MAKECPM.SUB in the last

frame, when you SUBMIT the command file. We can do this with symbolic parameters. The first symbolic parameter in a command file is indicated by $1; the second by $2, etc. We'll only need one to turn MAKECPM into a more flexible file.

```
PIP $1:=PIP.COM
PIP $1:=STAT.COM
PIP $1:=ED.COM
PIP $1:=SYSGEN.COM
```

Notice that the symbolic parameter $1 is used in place of a drive name. The actual parameter, a valid drive name, is supplied with the SUBMIT command like this:

```
SUBMIT MAKECPM B
```

This command will insert "B" wherever the first symbolic parameter appears in MAKECPM.SUB and execute the commands as if each specified drive B instead of $1. Notice that the command file follows each symbolic parameter with the colon (:) that is needed for a drivename. If the colon were omitted here it would need to be included in the SUBMIT command.

(a) What command could execute the command file MAKECPM, as shown above, copying the files onto drive C. ______________________

(b) Which element in MAKECPM.SUB above is a symbolic parameter? __________

(c) If a command file required two symbolic parameters, what would the name of the second one be? ______________________

(a) SUBMIT MAKECPM C; (b) $1; (c) $2

4. Command files can contain any combination of commands. Here is a list of commands that could be used to assemble a file of type ASM, erase any backup files, copy the PRN file produced by ASM to another drive and erase the original file.

```
ASM $1
ERA *.BAK
PIP $2:=$1.PRN
ERA $1.PRN
```

This file could be named ASSEMBLE.SUB. Two parameters are needed in the SUBMIT command to execute it. The first parameter is the filename of the program to be assembled. You only specify the first part, as it is always type ASM. The second names the drive on which you want to save the PRN file. Suppose the assembler language program is in file INVENT.ASM. You want the PRN file saved on drive B.

(a) Write a command to execute ASSEMBLE.SUB

A> ______________________

(b) Modify the file or the invoking command so the PRN file is printed rather than on drive B.

(a) SUBMIT ASSEMBLE INVENT B ; (b) change the PIP command to TYPE $1.PRN. You'll only need one parameter. To do this without changing the file, you could use SUBMIT ASSEMBLE INVENT LST.

5. Let's look at what actually happens when you enter a SUBMIT command. First of all, the system pairs any actual parameters in your SUBMIT command line with the symbolic parameters in the command file. If the numbers don't match, you'll get an error somewhere in the execution. If you have too few parameters in your SUBMIT statements, all symbolics are removed anyway. This generally results in an INVALID FORMAT. If you supply too many parameters, only the first ones are used to fill out the symbolics.

The submit function proceeds to create a file named $$$.SUB. This file contains all the commands with the actual parameters filled in. Suppose the command SUBMIT MAKECPM B were entered as in frame 3. The file $$$.SUB is created, using parameter B to replace $1 wherever it appears. The $$$.SUB file looks like this:

```
PIP B:=PIP.COM
PIP B:=STAT.COM
PIP B:=ED.COM
PIP B:=SYSGEN.COM
```

Then the SUBMIT program terminates and the system automatically reboots. After any warm or cold start the CCP will always read a $$$.SUB file on drive A instead of the console, so the commands in that file are processed. The last step of processing a $$$.SUB file is to erase it so control is returned to the console. Consider the file ASSEMBLE.SUB from the previous frame.

(a) What happens if you enter SUBMIT ASSEMBLE PROGRAM? ____________

(b) What is the name of the intermediate file created by CP/M?

(c) Write the contents of the intermediate file if you use SUBMIT ASSEMBLE PROGRAM B.

(d) When is the intermediate file processed?

____

(e) When is the intermediate file erased?

____

- - - - - - - - - - - - - - - - -

(a) some error will occur because you gave only one parameter. The error will be an INVALID FORMAT on PIP. ; (b) $$$.SUB;

(c)
```
ASM PROGRAM
ERA *.BAK
PIP B:=PROGRAM.PRN
ERA PROGRAM.PRN
```

(d) after the automatic reboot; (e) as the last step in processing the $$$.SUB file

6. Any $$$.SUB file on drive A has priority over the console and takes over whenever a cold or warm start is performed. If you SUBMIT a file from a disk other than A, the $$$.SUB file is created and stored on the originating disk. Control then returns to the CCP. Whenever that disk containing $$$.SUB is inserted into drive A, the next cold or warm start will begin processing it. The only way to prevent this from happening is to erase the $$$.SUB file from the disk before attempting to use the disk in drive A. At times, however, you may want to set up a file that will execute as soon as the system is booted from that disk. Suppose you want to immediately display a directory and the amount of space remaining on a disk when the system is booted. Assume you have a two-drive system.

(a) Write a file named DISPLAY.SUB.

____

____

____

(b) On which drive will you store DISPLAY.SUB?

____

(c) Write the SUBMIT command.

____

(d) Where is the $$$.SUB file stored?

____

(e) How can you execute $$$.SUB?

____

- - - - - - - - - - - - - - - - -

____

(a)
```
DIR
STAT
```

(b) drive B; (c) SUBMIT B:DISPLAY (if SUBMIT.COM is on disk B, you don't need the drive prefix); (d) on drive B; (e) boot with that disk in drive A

7. When you use SUBMIT, you may occassionally get effects you don't expect. Suppose, for example, you have a command file that copies all the files from disk A to disk B. The $$$.SUB file includes the command PIP B:=*.*. All the files will be copied to the B disk – including the $$$.SUB file! Then if you ever boot with the B disk, the SUB file will be processed immediately. We said earlier that SUBMIT removes the $$$.SUB file but only from the active or A disk. Recall that a $$$.SUB file can be processed only on the A disk.

Suppose a command file COPY.SUB includes these commands:

```
PIP $1=A:*.*
DIR $1:
STAT $1:
```

(a) How is the file executed for a copy to disk C?

(b) On what drive do you need the command file?

(c) After the SUBMIT program terminates normally, where will you have the $$$.SUB file?

(d) What sort of command, added to the file above, would eliminate the $$$.SUB file from the destination disk before the SUBMIT terminates.

- - - - - - - - - - - - - - -

(a) SUBMIT COPY C; (b) drive A; (c) on the C disk; (d) a command to erase it on $1 drive

8. When a $$$.SUB file is being processed, any error in a command will cause it to abort. However the $$$.SUB file remains there, ready to execute again when a warm or cold start occurs. If you erase the $$$.SUB file after any error, that won't happen. Many programs that run under CP/M erase any $$$.SUB files routinely, just in case. Sometimes it is interesting to TYPE a $$$.SUB file to help determine the cause of the error. Be sure to erase it before a cold or warm start is done. When a file has been submitted, command prompts and command lines are displayed on the console just as if you were interacting with the CCP.

You can interrupt processing of the file by pressing rubout (or delete) when a command is read and echoed. The result is to interrupt processing and to erase the $$$.SUB file. The timing is critical to interrupt SUBMIT processing. You need to press rubout when the A> prompt appears, just as a command is displayed.

(a) Under what circumstances might you find a $$$.SUB file in a disk directory?

____

____

____

(b) How can you interrupt processing of a SUBMIT command file?

____

____

(c) What will happen if you enter ERA $$$.SUB and there is no such file?

____

- - - - - - - - - - - - - - - -

(a) if you used SUBMIT on a drive other than A or if an error terminated processing; (b) push rubout when a command is displayed; (c) for version 2, the NO FILE message appears. No message appears for earlier versions. Nothing is erased in either case.

9. We've seen what happens when you use the SUBMIT command. Now let's take a closer look at the SUB file – what can you put into it and what it can do. We said that any CP/M commands, built-in or transient, can be used. Any command that invokes a COM file is valid. Any of the parameters can be replaced by symbolic parameters in the SUBMIT file. Normally a command line you enter at the console is processed by the CCP. Any parameters you can include in such a command line can be replaced with symbolic parameters and provided when the file is submitted.

You may want to store a dollar sign in a file to be submitted. Since the dollar sign character ($) generally indicates a symbolic parameter, you need to tell SUBMIT if it means something else. You do this by using a double dollar sign ($$) which SUBMIT reduces to a single one. For example, to erase a file named THANK.$$$ from within a SUBMIT command file, you write one of these commands:

```
ERA THANK.$$*
ERA THANK.$$$$$$
```

You do not use ERA THANK.$$$, as SUBMIT cannot relate that to the file.

Suppose MIXTURE.SUB contains these four lines:

```
ERA $1:*.DAT
$3
PIP $1:=*.DAT[$2]
REN KEEP.SUB=SUB.$$$
```

The command SUBMIT MIXTURE B U Y is issued.

(a) Why is symbolic parameter $3 invalid?

____

(b) Rewrite the last line so it is valid.

____

(c) Suppose the command file contains only the last two lines – corrected. Write a command to execute it using the B disk as the destination. Specify that all characters will be converted to lower case on the B disk.

____

(d) How will you be able to find the data in SUB.$$$ after the CCP regains control?

____

- - - - - - - - - - - - - - -

(a) it doesn't represent a parameter; (b) REN KEEP.SUB=SUB.$$*;
(c) SUBMIT MIXTURE B L; (d) it is still in KEEP.SUB

10. At times you may need to store a control character in a command file. The ED program, along with most other text editors and word processors, processes control characters as it encounters them. In a SUBMIT command file you can store control characters by entering an up-arrow (↑) or a caret (ˆ), whichever your terminal has, followed by the alphabetic character. When a command file is being processed, SUBMIT interprets the sequence caret-letter or up-arrow-letter as the appropriate control character.

(a) How could you put control-C into a SUBMIT file? ______________

(b) Could you use a caret as a caret in a SUBMIT file? ______________

- - - - - - - - - - - - - - -

(a) caret-C or up-arrow-C; (b) no; it introduces a control character

11. We've been dealing with commands that use only parameter input and run to completion without any other console interaction. Often we need to use commands that require some type of line input from the console. Line input for the CP/M transient commands and other COM files can be handled by storing them on separate lines in a SUB file under version 2.0. The console interaction will be just the same as if you

entered the command individually. All the commands and line inputs are displayed as the file is processed so you can tell where the system is in the process. The console screen looks just as it does when the commands are entered one at a time. Built-in commands are different. When the separate command ERA *.* is issued, the question ALL FILES? (Y/N) is displayed. Versions earlier than 2.0 handle this in a SUB file. SUBMIT deserts you after the line entry or tries to use the next line as a response. Under version 2.0, this can be handled in a SUB file.

(a) Which of the CP/M commands below is likely to require some line input?

______ ED NEW.FIL

______ ERA *.COM

______ SYSGEN

______ MOVCPM

______ STAT *.*

(b) Suppose you are executing a command file and see this displayed:

A>PIP B:=STAT.COM

What must you do? ______________________________

(c) Suppose you see this displayed:

```
A>ERA *.*
ALL FILES? (Y/N)_
```

What must you do to erase all the files? ______________________

(a) ED, SYSGEN, MOVCPM in 2.0; (b) nothing, just wait; (c) type Y and enter (then you'll be out of SUBMIT)

12. Let's look at a complete screen display and interaction under SUBMIT. Suppose COPY.SUB contains these commands:

```
SYSGEN
PIP $1:=A:*.*
ERA $1:$$*.SUB
DIR $1:
```

You enter SUBMIT COPY B to execute the file. You then see this on the screen (the A> prompt comes up first, then the rest).

```
A>SYSGEN
SYSGEN VER 2.2
SOURCE DRIVE NAME (OR RETURN TO SKIP)_
```

You enter A, and see:

```
SOURCE ON A, THEN TYPE RETURN_
```

(a) What do you enter now? ______________________

(b) You see this:

```
FUNCTION COMPLETE
DESTINATION DRIVE NAME (OR RETURN TO REBOOT)_
```

What do you enter? ______________________

(c) You see this:

```
DESTINATION ON B, THEN TYPE RETURN_
```

What do you enter? ______________________

(d) You see this:

```
FUNCTION COMPLETE
DESTINATION DRIVE NAME (OR RETURN TO REBOOT)_
```

What do you enter? ______________________

- - - - - - - - - - - - - - - -

(a) <CR>; (b) b; (c) <CR> if the disk is in b; (d) <CR>

13. Let's continue with the execution of COPY.SUB. The last <CR> you entered for SYSGEN terminates SYSGEN input and the system proceeds automatically to the next command. You see this:

```
A>PIP B:=A:*.*

COPYING_
```

The list of files copied is displayed on your screen.

(a) What is displayed next? A> ______________________

(b) Then what? A> ______________________

(c) What is the final display resulting from the COPY command file?

____

- - - - - - - - - - - - - - - -

(a) A>ERA B:$*.SUB (the $$ has been reduced); (b) A>DIR B: ;

(c) the directory from disk B

14. The SUBMIT command by itself doesn't handle line input, as we've seen. Version 2 of CP/M provides a command XSUB that you can use in a command file. XSUB can handle most line input so you can include appropriate responses in your command file. However the line entries cannot be made symbolic in the file. When you use XSUB as the first command in the file, the SUBMIT file reads many line entries from the file instead of from the console. Suppose this is SCRATCH.SUB:

```
XSUB
ERA $1:*.*
Y
STAT $1
```

When SUBMIT SCRATCH B is entered, the SUB.$$$ file is created. You see this information on the console:

```
A>XSUB
A>ERA B:*.*
ALL? (Y/N)Y
A>STAT B:
stat line
```

Without XSUB you would not be able to include the line entry Y in the file, and in fact, couldn't reliably include ERA *.* at all.

(a) Which command handles symbolic parameters? ______________________

(b) Which command handles line entries? ______________________

(c) In a command file, where does XSUB go? ______________________

(d) Can you use a symbolic parameter to represent a line entry in a command file?

____

- - - - - - - - - - - - - - - -

(a) SUBMIT; (b) XSUB; (c) first entry; (d) no

15. The CP/M disk (Version 2.0 and later) includes XSUB.COM. This is a separate program but it has no effect when run alone. As the first command in a submit file, XSUB extends the power of SUBMIT so that it can process line input to programs as well as commands to the CCP. When you use XSUB, it processes the file instead of SUBMIT. You still need SUBMIT to begin the process.

When XSUB is used, it remains in memory even after the command file has been processed. Each time a warm start is performed, the message (xsub active) is displayed on the terminal. XSUB doesn't interfere with most CP/M operations. However if you submit another file, XSUB will take over even if no XSUB is included in the command file. The only way to get rid of XSUB is to cold start the system.

(a) Suppose you see the message (xsub active). You need to PIP a file to drive A. What must you do first?

____

____

(b) Suppose you enter SUBMIT RUNIT when you have just cold started the system. The file RUNIT.SUB includes line input for some of the programs. Write the first command line in the file. ______________________

(c) Under what circumstances could you process RUNIT.SUB without that first line?

____

- - - - - - - - - - - - - - - -

(a) nothing; XSUB won't interfere; (b) XSUB; (c) if (xsub active) appears on the console

16. We said you can include line input to most programs in a SUB file with XSUB. There is one type of line input you can't include and that's the plain carriage return. As you know, SYSGEN requires a carriage return for many responses. These responses can't be included in a SUB file. As in SUB files without XSUB, the console will return to you for SYSGEN input.

The continuing PIP format is terminated by a single carriage return. This also must be handled individually.

Here is a command file that includes examples:

```
XSUB
ERA $1:*.*
Y
SYSGEN
PIP $1:=*.COM
STAT $1:*.*
```

(a) Which command will require console line input from you?

____

(b) Which command is followed by its line input?

____

(c) Modify the file so it will create a maximum size CP/M for the system rather than copying it. Write the command and indicate where it would be inserted.

command: ______________________

insert: ______________________

(d) Will this require any other changes in the SUB file? ______________________

(e) Will it require any changes to your line input demands? ______________________

____

- - - - - - - - - - - - - - - -

(a) SYSGEN; (b) ERA; (c) MOVCPM * *, before SYSGEN; (d) no;
(e) you'll need to enter Y or <CR> for MOVCPM, and <CR> to skip the source drive for SYSGEN

17. After XSUB is initiated it remains active. If you submit another file that includes the XSUB command, you'll receive the message "Extended submit already active," and the file proceeds to execute. If you submit a file that doesn't use XSUB, it will be treated as though it includes XSUB. It may not pause for line input from the console. You'll want to assume XSUB for all your command files if you use it at all.

Another caution is using command files in general has to do with changing drives or user numbers. You may very easily get separated from your $$$.SUB file and it won't be able to continue processing. However it will still be there on the A disk, ready to take over again when you return there under the original user number. It's safest to avoid changing the active drive or user number from within a SUBMIT file.

(a) Suppose you changed drives with a symbolic parameter in a command file. The system returns control to you on the B drive. What can you do about the $$$.SUB file on A drive? ______________________________

(b) Suppose you changed user numbers on disk A and the system returns control to you on that user number. What can you do about the $$$.SUB file?

____

(c) Suppose you see the message (xsub active) and submit a file that includes XSUB. What effect will this have?

____

(d) Suppose you see the message (xsub active) and submit a file that doesn't include XSUB but does need line input (not blank lines). Will it run correctly?

____

— — — — — — — — — — — — — — — —

(a) ERA A:$$$.SUB; (b) change to another drive, return to original user number, then ERA A:$$$.SUB; (c) message (Extended submit already active), but no effect on file processing; (d) probably not, depending on line input needs

18. Routine editing is a useful application of SUBMIT files only for upper case characters; the program converts everything to upper case. Suppose you have twenty files in which you have used the term BX-12. You can create a submit file to change all references from BX-12 to 12-BX. Write a command file to do this using a macro under ED. You'll be able to submit the command file with each filename as an actual parameter.

____

____

____

____

____

____

\- - - - - - - - - - - - - - - -

```
XSUB
ED $1
#A
MNBX-12^Z-5DI12-BX^Z
E
```

19. To build the previous command file you'll have to use a caret or up-arrow as your control character indicator. The E is essential. If you omit E, the system will wait until you enter it from the keyboard. Before you SUBMIT a command file that includes line input, its a good idea to enter the commands separately to make sure you have accounted for all the line input.

When the SUBMIT is entered, you'll see all the prompts and responses displayed on the screen. If an error occurs in any command processing the SUBMIT is interrupted. You'll be able to tell from your console what was completed. If you see a message that doesn't cause an interrupt, you may want to terminate SUBMIT yourself.

(a) How can you terminate SUBMIT processing?

____

(b) How can you terminate XSUB control?

____

\- - - - - - - - - - - - - - - -

(a) rubout when CCP prompt (A>) is displayed; (b) cold start

Any CP/M commands (COM file references) can be included in SUBMIT files. You can even include a SUBMIT command as the last command in a SUB file. This allows you to chain separate groups of commands. However you should not try such a technique until you are at ease with the un-chained SUBMIT.

You have seen how to use SUBMIT for batch processing of CP/M commands. You've seen how XSUB lets you include line input to programs as well as the CP/M commands in a SUB file. You'll get a chance to build and execute a command file in the suggested machine exercises for this chapter.

CHAPTER 10 SELF-TEST

1. Write a command file named FIXUP.SUB that will accomplish the following on the originating disk.

   (a) Rename the BAK file of an symbolic filename to have filetype OLD.
   (b) Erase all BAK files.
   (c) Display the disk status.

2. Write a command to process the file you created in question 1 saving PERSNL.BAK file as PERSNL.OLD.

3. What would you expect to happen if you omit the symbolic parameter in the SUBMIT command?

4. Assuming you entered a valid SUBMIT command, write out the contents of the temporary file.

5. What is the name of this temporary file? ______

6. Suppose you create FIXUP.SUB on drive B and submit it from there. When will the commands be executed?

7. Write a command file to accomplish the following:

   - Erase all files on the specified drive. (Symbolic parameter for drivename.)
   - Construct a maximum size CP/M and place it on the system tracks of the specified drive.
   - Copy all files (including system files) from the A disk to the specified drive.
   - Remove the temporary SUB file from the specified drive.
   - Display a directory and status of the specified drive.

8. Suppose you file from question 7 is named BACKUP.SUB and you wish to use it to duplicate your disk onto drive C. Write the command.

9. Consider the file you wrote in question 7 above. Which commands require that *you* make some line input from the console?

10. Suppose your last four lines in the BACKUP.SUB file look like this:

```
$1:
ERA $$*.SUB
DIR
STAT
```

What will happen when the *first* line shown here is executed?

Will processing continue?

11. What command should you issue before returning to the A disk?

Chapter 10 Answer Key

1.
```
REN $1.OLD=$1.BAK
ERA *.BAK
STAT
```

2. `SUBMIT FIXUP PERSNL`

3. An error in processing the REN command. (INVALID FORMAT)

4.
```
REN PERSNL.OLD=PERSNL.BAK
ERA *.BAK
STAT
```

5. `$$$.SUB`

6. When that disk is inserted in drive A and the system is booted.

7.
```
XSUB
ERA $1:*.*
MOVCPM * *
SYSGEN
PIP $1=A:*.*[R]
ERA $1:$$*.SUB
DIR $1:
STAT $1:
```

8. `SUBMIT BACKUP C`

9. `MOVCPM` and `SYSGEN`

10. Control will switch to the specified drive (C). Processing will stop.

11. `ERA A:$$$.SUB`

Suggested Machine Exercises

Before you begin this exercise make sure that you have a disk containing SUBMIT.COM and XSUB.COM, if you have version 2.0 or later. The same disk should contain PRACTICE.1 which you edited in the last chapter. You can PIP it over if necessary. Convert it to all upper case if PRACTICE.1 isn't in that form already. You'll need a scratch disk with nothing important on it, as well.

1. For the first exercise use ED to build FIXUP.SUB containing the commands you wrote for Self-Test question 1.

   SUBMIT that file to save PRACTICE.BAK as PRACTICE.OLD and get rid of other BAK files.

Be sure this is working successfully before you continue with the other exercises.

2. For the second exercise use ED to build BACKUP.SUB, which you wrote in Self-Test question 7. (If you don't have version 2.0 or later, eliminate XSUB and ERA $1:*.*.)

   Most important: be sure to put the symbolic parameter in the ERA command or you'll do terrible things to the data on your A disk!

   Submit that file for drive B. Be sure you have a dispensable disk in drive B before you SUBMIT the file.

   If you get errors, re-edit the file to clean up the commands. Boot with the new disk to make sure it worked.

3. Finally, create a SUB file to edit PRACTICE.1. We want to change every occurrence of PRACTICE to TRIAL. Put all your line input in the file.

   Then submit the file. Examine PRACTICE.1 to see if it works.

POSTWORD

This completes our self-teaching guide on CP/M. You've learned how to use all the built-in commands and most of the transient commands. We've omitted the commands that pertain specifically to 8080 Assembler programming. Appendix C contains a summary of all the commands you've studied in this book. We suggest you cut out Appendix C and keep it near your console.

Good Luck!

APPENDIX A

Changing Device Assignments

If your CP/M system has been altered so that you can make device assignments from the console using STAT, these are the commands you can use:

1. STAT DEV:

    This command will display the current device assignments.

2. STAT logical=physical, . . .

    This command changes one or more device assignments. For example, to change the console from CRT: to TTY:, enter STAT CON:=TTY:. To change both CON: and LST: to TTY:, enter STAT CON:=TTY:,LST:=TTY:.

The permitted physical device names are:

Consoles

TTY: Teletype-style terminal

CRT: Cathode-ray tube terminal (video terminal)

BAT: Used for batch mode processing – that is, no operator interaction. Input is RDR:. All output is sent to LST:

UCI: User-defined console

Listing Devices

TTY:

CRT:

LPT: Line printer

ULI: User defined listing terminal

Readers

TTY:	
PTR:	Paper tape reader or any high speed reader
UR1: UR2:	User defined readers

Punches

TTY:	
PTP:	Paper tape punch or any high speed output device
UP1: UP2:	User defined punches

APPENDIX B

PIP Parameters

*B	–	Block mode transfer; transfers blocks of data signaled by ^S character.
Dn	–	Delete characters after column n.
E	–	Echo on console.
F	–	Filter form feeds.
*H	–	Transfer and check hex data; remove unnecessary characters and display errors on console.
*I	–	Ignore :00 records in H type transfer. (I implies H so don't use both.)
L	–	Translate letters to lower case.
N	–	Add line numbers.
N2	–	Add line numbers and expand all tabs to the next eighth column.
*O	–	Object file transfer; ignore normal end of file.
Pn	–	Insert form feed every n lines; if n is omitted, 60 is assumed.
Qstring^Z	–	Quit copying after string.
Sstring^Z	–	Start copying with string.
Tn	–	Expand tab characters to every nth column.
U	–	Translate letters to upper case.
*V	–	Read new file to verify.
*Z	–	Zero parity bit on input.

* Not covered in this book.

APPENDIX C

Reference Summary

[( ) indicates optional parameters]

BUILT-IN COMMANDS

ERA filename<CR> – Erase named file/s
DIR (filename)<CR> – Display directory of file/s
REN new-specific-filename=old-specific-filename<CR> – Change name of file
SAVE pages specific-filename<CR> – Store pages as file
TYPE specific-filename<CR> – Display file
USER user-number<CR> – Change user areas in Version 2

TRANSIENT COMMANDS

ASM specific-filename<CR> – Assemble ASM file (omit type from filename)
DDT (specific-filename)<CR> – Debug COM or HEX file; Pull into TPA
DUMP specific-filename<CR> – Print dump listing of file
LOAD specific-filename<CR> – Make COM file from HEX file (omit type from filename)

MOVCPM (n / *) (*)<CR> – Construct system of size nK bytes
PIP<CR> – Initiate PIP program and return command prompt
PIP destination=source(,source2, etc.) ([parameters])<CR> – Copy source file/s to destination file/s

STAT filename ($R/W / $R/O / $DIR / $SYS / $S) <CR> – Display/change status of file/s

STAT (d: / VAL: / DEV: / DSK: / USR:) <CR> – Display status of indicated device

STAT logical=physical(,logical=physical, etc.)<CR> – change device assignment/s
SUBMIT specific-filename (parameters)<CR> – execute SUB file (omit type from filename)
SYSGEN<CR> – initiate SYSGEN program and display instructions

ED COMMANDS AND CP/M CONTROL CHARACTERS BELOW.

PIP PARAMETERS ARE SHOWN IN APPENDIX B.

ED COMMANDS

ED specific-filename (drivename)<CR>

nA –	append n lines
±B –	move character pointer to beginning or end
±nC –	move character pointer n characters
±nD –	delete n characters
E –	save file and end ED
Fstring –	find string
H –	save file and restart ED
I<CR> –	enter insert level
Istring^Z –	insert string
Istring<CR> –	insert string and <CR><LF>

Jsearch-string^Zinsert-string^Zdelete-string<CR> – juxtapose and delete

±nK –	Kill n lines
±nL –	move character pointer n lines
nM –	execute macro n times
Nstring –	extended find string
O –	return to original file
±nP –	display pages
Q –	quit
R –	read temporary LIB file

Rspecific-filename – read LIB file (omit type from filename)

Sdelete-string^Zinsert-string – substitute

±nT –	type n lines
±U –	upper case translation
±V –	line numbering
nW –	write n lines
nX –	append n lines to temporary LIB file
nZ –	sleep n seconds
±n –	move n lines and type
n: –	move to line n
:n –	through line n

CP/M CONTROL CHARACTERS

^C –	reboot
^E –	start new line
^H –	backspace
^I –	tab
^J –	line feed
^L –	substitute <CR><LF>
^M –	return
^P –	echo print
^R –	reshow line
^S –	interrupt output
^U –	delete line
^X –	delete line
^Z –	string terminator
delete/rubout –	delete and display previous character

Index